# THE ESSENTIAL

## *FAMILY CAMPER*

# THE ESSENTIAL

# FAMILY

# CAMPER

## A Handbook for the Great Outdoors

## ZORA AIKEN
## AND DAVID AIKEN

RAGGED MOUNTAIN PRESS / McGRAW-HILL

CAMDEN, MAINE • NEW YORK • SAN FRANCISCO • LISBON • LONDON
MADRID • MEXICO CITY • MILAN • NEW DELHI • SAN JUAN
SEOUL • SINGAPORE • SYDNEY • TORONTO

ALSO IN THE RAGGED MOUNTAIN PRESS ESSENTIAL SERIES
*The Essential Backpacker: A Complete Guide for the Foot Traveler*, Adrienne Hall
*The Essential Cross-Country Skier: A Step-by-Step Guide*, Paul Petersen
   and Richard A. Lovett
*The Essential Outdoor Gear Manual: Equipment Care, Repair, and Selection*,
   2nd edition, Annie Getchell and Dave Getchell Jr.
*The Essential Sea Kayaker: A Complete Guide for the Open-Water Paddler*,
   2nd edition, David Seidman
*The Essential Snowshoer: A Step-by-Step Guide*, Marianne Zwosta
*The Essential Touring Cyclist,* 2nd edition, Richard A. Lovett
*The Essential Whitewater Kayaker: A Complete Course,* Jeff Bennett
*The Essential Wilderness Navigator*, 2nd edition, David Seidman and Paul Cleveland

**Ragged Mountain Press**
*A Division of The McGraw-Hill Companies*

10 9 8 7 6 5 4 3 2 1
Copyright © 1996, 2001 Zora and David Aiken

*Library of Congress Cataloging-in-Publication Data*
   Aiken, Zora.
     The essential family camper : a handbook for the great outdoors / Zora Aiken
   and David Aiken ; Drawings by David Aiken.—2nd ed.
       p.     cm. — (Ragged Mountain Press essential series)
   Rev. ed. of: Simple tent camping. c1996.
   Includes index.
     ISBN 0-07-137614-3
     1. Camping. 2. Tents. 3. Camping—Equipment and supplies. I. Aiken,
   David, 1940– II. Aiken, Zora. Simple tent camping. III. Title. IV. Essential series
   (Camden, Me.)
     GV191.7.A39 2001
     796.54—dc21                                              2001002423

Questions regarding the content of this book should be addressed to
Ragged Mountain Press
P.O. Box 220
Camden, ME 04843
www.raggedmountainpress.com

Questions regarding the ordering of this book should be addressed to
The McGraw-Hill Companies
Customer Service Department
P.O. Box 547
Blacklick, OH 43004
Retail customers: 1-800-262-4729
Bookstores: 1-800-722-4726

This book is printed on 70 lb. Citation by R. R. Donnelley, Crawfordsville, IN
Design by Dede Cummings
Production by PerfecType, Dan Kirchoff, and Janet Robbins
Edited by Jonathan Eaton, Jane Crosen, and Pamela Benner
Illustrations by David Aiken

To our parents,

for instilling an appreciation for nature
and a love for the outdoors.

# CONTENTS

# ACKNOWLEDGMENTS

Camping is an ongoing learning experience, with the how-to closely connected to the why. We've met teachers everywhere, while kayak camping in Quetico or canoeing in the Everglades; from Assateague beaches to the Smoky Mountains.

We want to acknowledge the example left us by Mom (everybody's Aunt Peggy) and by Grandpa Fredrickson; each brought humor and a sense of discovery to every new place, every time.

We learned much about wildlife and nature's ways from Magnus Nyman, a true outdoorsman who practiced conservation and habitat restoration, and who shared his knowledge and experience with hundreds of lucky listeners.

**For specific camping hints, we thank:**
Ken and Donna Aiken (and Michel and Ed), who shared their fun and their family with us.

Bob Umphrey ("Pop"), for always finding the best of autumn's color, and for capturing so many camping moments on film.

Bill, Diane, Ted, and Tracey Biggs, who showed us the Ontario wilderness adventures of island camping, shore lunching, and rapids shooting.

Drew, Jocelyn, and Jordyn Beck, for the up-close look at "baby-in-the-woods."

Mike and Tammy Jaggi, who, along with Knucklehead and Freda, find fun (or bring it) whatever the situation.

Jerry and Judy MacNab: sailors, backpackers, whitewater rafters, whose spirit of adventure never quits.

Jon Phipps, an enthusiastic hiker with a sincere concern for wilderness preservation.

Mike Fritz, Christopher Lee, Tom Franko, Joe Rulli, Patrick McLaughlin, and Dan Fuerbringer, for photographs from their backcountry camping.

Thanks to the people at Ragged Mountain Press:

Jonathan Eaton, editorial director, for guidance through a lengthy evolution.

Alan Kesselheim, technical editor, for technical help and content critique.

# INTRODUCTION

If your typical week seems marked in double time, come Friday you want—you need—a time out. Make that time outdoors—a great way to back away from the blur of life in the express lane.

You don't need to travel far to find a different world, but you will need to change your way of living, at least temporarily, because the best way to experience all the good of the outdoors is to plant a tent in its midst. Here, you'll wake up to dawn colors mirrored in a shimmering pond, or sunbeams flickering across the forest floor. You'll tune to nature's sounds: wind humming a lullaby, birds chattering in chorus, crickets adding percussion.

You could seek all this good input for just your own benefit, but it's all the better when shared with the significant others in your life.

Tent campers give all sorts of reasons why they like outdoor living. It's a return to a simpler life, or a simple change of pace. It's a challenge of self-sufficiency, or a get-together with friends. Some try to define it in more cerebral terms, like filling the voids in life with beauty or serenity, freedom or space, but it all comes down to feeling good, because that's what camping does for you.

Besides the basic fun of living outdoors, camping provides time and opportunity for individual interests as diverse as fish, rocks, or stars. Camping's good for families, too, whether the particular adventure is a nontraditional honeymoon or an annual vacation for grandparents and grandchildren. Adults enjoy watching the outdoor experience through a child's eye, renewing all the discovery and joy that "firsts" always bring. Children learn hands-on and hands-off about environmental sensitivity and nature preservation; often, young campers grow into dedicated conservationists.

If you're just starting this soon-to-be tradition in your family, this book can help you ease into the camping life. Wilderness surroundings may be your eventual goal, but start camping within the structure of an organized campground. Don't consider the challenge of a canoe trip for your first ventures—camping by car is the more sensible beginning. Think simple: rent a simple-to-pitch tent, pick a simple-to-find campground, and take simple-to-prepare food. Then take nature's course, and discover a whole new world of fun.

Note: The brand names mentioned in *The Essential Family Camper* are popular with many who provided information for the book, but their inclusion is not meant to suggest those brands are the only or the best products for a particular use.

Equipment comparison is not the focus of this book. Manufacturer's reputation, product longevity, and old-fashioned word-of-mouth are all good sources for product recommendation. Talk to experienced campers.

# THE
# CAMPSITE

# *TENT TYPES*

## 1

While you can adapt household items for a lot of camping gear, a functional tent would be difficult to make from anything you might find hiding in the storage shed. For your initial forays into the outdoor world, your weekend home will be borrowed from a friend or rented from an outfitter, but once your family gets hooked on camping you'll want and need your own. Tempting though it may be, this is not the place to cut too many corners; your enjoyment of the outdoors starts with and depends on the most basic of creature comforts: you must be able to stay dry and keep warm. (And don't think too much about king-size beds or innerspring mattresses, and you won't be too disappointed.)

In ordinary, comfortable indoor life, you don't think about how a wall or a roof shelters you, nor what they shelter you from. Climatic considerations are confined to opening or closing a window or adjusting the temperature level of heater or air conditioner. The weather report is just part of the evening news; you can always stay inside if a storm is coming.

Outdoor living, however, raises some questions. What constitutes adequate shelter? How do tents provide it? How much space is enough? Before parting with your dollars, you'll want to know as much as possible about tent design, construction, and detailing, so you can make a good choice for your needs.

## COMMON GROUND

Different tent designs suit different applications. Which style you eventually buy will depend to a large extent on how you want to use the tent, but certain considerations are common to all. These can be used as a starting point in your search for shelter, and as a later basis for comparing individual tents.

As a logical first, the tent must stay dry inside, even when a summer squall sends rain into camp at a near-horizontal angle. The floor must halt any upward absorption of ground moisture; if the tent fails to achieve either of the above requirements, the campers will not stay happy very long.

Good ventilation is the next necessity. The tent should have openings (doors or windows) on all sides, if practical, to catch breezes from any direction and carry condensation away. Fine-meshed screens on all windows and doorways let air in and keep bugs out. Covering flaps of tent fabric roll down to cover the window screening if the breeze turns chilly or if you want some privacy.

Ideally, a tent should be fairly easy to put up (pitch) or take down (strike), even in the dark and especially in the rain. It should fold into a compact, easily carried package, usually in its own storage bag, ready to stuff into a car or canoe.

While the backpacker or bicyclist must count every ounce and inch, the car or canoe camper can handle the added weight and mass of a larger, more comfortable tent. (Size may be most critical when you're tent-bound by an all-day rain. You should be able to assign a corner where each person can read, nap, play, or otherwise hide from the weather.)

Don't expect a tent to keep you truly warm on truly cold days; it can only give protection from wind and wetness. (Tent heaters are an iffy option; see page 39.) Don't be put off by thoughts of rain and cold; the idea is to prepare for the worst-case

*Though not always possible, it's most convenient to be able to drive into the tent site in order to unload (and reload) the car.*

days so you can enjoy the best ones. With summer-time camping, cold is seldom a problem.

# THEMES AND VARIATIONS

If your personal experience with tents is limited to a childhood Scout outing, supplemented by videos of arctic exploration, then a trip to a camping outfitter or a browse through a tent equipment catalog is appropriate. Not to buy—not yet—but just to look and learn.

Tents are made in a surprising number of shapes and sizes. Your first look may create more confusion than clarification, but you'll soon see that tents can be sorted into a few basic shapes (except for the variety of oddly shaped small tents made for the specialty niche of lightweight backpacking gear, a category the car camping family can happily ignore). Consider the basic possibilities and what you intend to do with your tent.

Will you stay in one place for a week at a time, or move to a different location every day? Where will you camp: in shaded forests, or on exposed beaches or rocky hills? What time of year will you do most of your camping? (Some tents are rated as three-season, some as four-season tents; unless you plan to go mountain climbing in January, don't bother looking at a four-season tent.)

Size is defined by a number of factors, including shape, center height, floor square footage (look at usable floor space relative to straight or sloping walls), and the number of campers that should be able to sleep in the tent. Unless your family is munchkin size, don't believe the numbers ratings. Mentally remove at least one person from the advertised sleeping capacity. One way to judge size requirement is to make a floor plan grid and position the appropriate number of sleeping bag shapes inside (allow extra space for gear). Car campers will be able to add more elbow room.

For your early tenting trips, try to borrow or rent two or three different styles so you can start to see the differences. For the typical family weekend outing, you'll be looking at four basic designs: A-frame, dome, umbrella, and cabin/wall.

## A-Frame Tent

With a low profile, this variation on the classic pup tent sheds wind much better than a tent with vertical walls. Some A-frames are freestanding; they can be set up without ground stakes or guylines, an advantage if you want to move the tent after it's assembled.

The simple design of A-frames allows them to be pitched, packed, and carried easily, but their shape minimizes space inside. A modified version

with a short vertical wall section has more usable floor space, suitable for a couple camping with a toddler.

The A-frame can be as basic as tent fabric draped over a line strung between two trees. Lacking tree support, it can be set up with a single pole holding up the tent center at each end, and corners staked out in the A. Newer, freestanding designs use A-shaped poles at each end, held together by a tension bar/ridgepole across the top.

Note that if a tent is freestanding, it can also be freemoving, and will do just that in a good wind. Always stake down the tent once you've settled on a good site.

## Dome Tent

Whether described as a modified dome, square dome, rectangular dome, or geodesic dome, all dome tents suggest the classic shape of a proven shelter—the Eskimo igloo.

Self-supported (freestanding), they can be set up on rocky ground or wooden platforms, but they, too, should be staked or weighted down in some way to prevent a dramatic escape.

The arched walls of a dome tent are closer to vertical than the A-frame's wedge, so more floor

with rain fly

*The A-frame tent.*

*The dome tent has been a popular style for years—lightweight, easy to set up, and movable.*

gonal geodesic dome is the best wind resistor, hence the most stable tent. One minor disadvantage: if the wind catches the fabric as you're in the process of setting up, your dome wants to fly away. On a normal, calm day, it's an easy setup.

## Umbrella Tent

This design is a very livable compromise between the space-limiting curve of a dome style and the wide-open interior of a cabin tent. Also self-supporting (freestanding), the umbrella's high side walls allow use of all floor space, and the headroom extends well beyond the center. With a slight angle to the walls, the umbrella is better able to withstand wind than the straight-walled cabin tent.

Unlike their namesake, umbrella tents are easy to put up, and they hold their shape, even in windy conditions. Most have a built-in front awning section, for a convenient covered porch.

Families with older children often use two umbrella tents rather than a single larger cabin tent. The umbrellas are set up face to face, so the connected awnings form a camper's breezeway. The children like the independence of their separate room, and the parents like the privacy and relative quiet of theirs.

space is usable for sleeping bags and duffels. There's enough headroom in the center to reduce the risk of the semipermanent slouch developed by campers with less flexible back muscles.

With no large, flat surfaces exposed to wind, the dome shape is able to shed gusts well; a hexa-

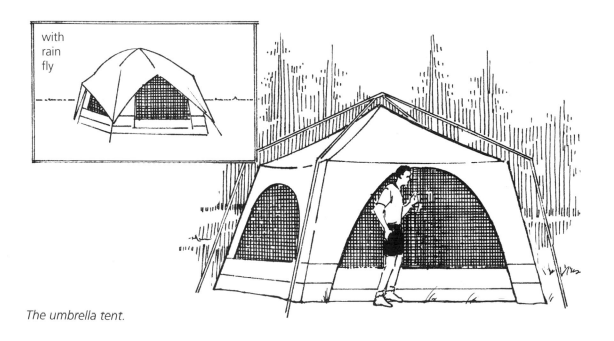

with rain fly

*The umbrella tent.*

one room

two rooms

Floor plans

removable fabric divider

*The cabin tent.*

# Tent Tips

### Think Before You Look

- If your someday plan includes canoe camping, consider the weight/size factor before purchasing a tent.
- Even if you plan to do only car camping, you can't always drive the car to the actual campsite; you may have to carry gear some distance, so don't discount the weight factor completely. A 9- or 10-foot-square dome or cabin-style tent is a decent size for a couple with two children, yet it's still fairly easy to handle.
- Advantages of a freestanding tent: you can pick it up to move it, or to shake out an accumulation of debris.
- Consider ease of setting up and taking down the tent, especially with kids.
- If you're camping with young children, a two-room tent gives everybody the most security, while retaining some privacy. Later, older children may prefer a separate tent; each family will know when that age line is crossed.
- Even if you use a second tent for the children, be sure the whole family can fit into the main tent on those occasions when a sudden urge for family togetherness is prompted by a lightning display.

### Color Considerations

- At one time, color choice for a tent was khaki or camouflage. Today, you can either blend with nature or make a fashion statement.
- One reason for a bright-colored tent: a small child can more easily recognize "home" in an ordinary campground situation; if the child should wander away from a wilderness camp, a spot of color could be an eye-catcher.
- Remember that dark colors absorb more sun (think heat) and light colors reflect it, keeping the tent cooler.
- Curiously, one study indicated darker colors are more resistant to ultraviolet light.

### Look Before You Buy

- Get recommendations from as many sources as you can find. Talk to other campers, outfitters and suppliers, and manufacturers.
- Look at the way a tent is sewn. Puckers might indicate the possibility of excessive strain, a tear waiting to happen. Look for bartacking at stress points and flaps over zipper tracks.
- If a seam is in contact with wet

## Cabin Tent

As its name suggests, the cabin tent (or wall tent) is most like a familiar house or cottage shape. Cabin tents have good headroom throughout, and the most interior volume. With vertical walls, you can set up bunk cots, if need be. Some models are divided into two rooms, and some include an attached screen room.

Cabin tents require more support poles than other styles, so setup is a bit more involved. You probably wouldn't want to set up and take down a cabin tent on a daily basis, but for long weekends and vacation weeks when traveling by car, a cabin style is the tent of choice, for personal comfort and for storage space.

Since they are the largest tent type, they're also the heaviest. Their high, straight walls can be a problem in high winds, so you must set poles and/or tie lines carefully. Also, unless you add a sep-

arate tarp over the top of the tent (and extending beyond the side walls), you must cover the windows when it rains, temporarily cutting off most of your ventilation.

# CONSTRUCTION

## Overhead

New campers are surprised to learn that many tent roofs are not waterproof, since that would seem to be the first line of defense against wet weather. The thinking is correct, but the rain is kept off the tent roof by a separate piece of waterproof fabric called the rain fly.

When people spend time in a small tent, moisture is released into the air from wet clothes, damp bodies, or normal breathing. If that moisture were to reach the inside surface of a waterproof tent ceiling, it could condense and rain back down onto

## Tent Tips (continued)

ground, leaks are almost guaranteed. Tub-style floors prevent them.

- Look for reinforcements in the fabric at stress points: corners, ring attachments, zippers, etc.
- On a good seam, the fabric is rolled over, then taped, not simply stitched.
- Most waterproofing is done with one or more coatings of polyurethane. At least one manufacturer treats the fabric with both polyurethane and silicone.
- A decent manufacturer's warranty is a good indication of a company's confidence in its own product.
- For your first tent, look for an outfitter who sells used gear. Also check classifieds in outdoor magazines and larger city newspapers.
- You might see a used tent at a

flea market or garage sale, but if poles are missing, think twice about buying it, or be prepared to do some custom pole-fitting. If the tent is more than a few years old, you may not find exact replacement poles—or other fittings that may be missing.

- When comparing tents, analyze the differences in price. Detailing can help separate good from best; manufacturer's reputation is another indicator. Camping outfitters usually have hands-on experience with equipment and can offer follow-up service and advice that discount chain stores cannot.
- While fiberglass poles may not be quite as strong as aluminum, they also do not share aluminum's attraction for lightning. In the extremely unlikely

event that lightning should hit a tree near your tent, it *could* side-flash to aluminum tent poles.

### A Few Cautions

- Don't spritz stiff or sticky zippers with an oily lubricant; it will stain the fabric and possibly damage it. Instead, use plain wax or bar soap.
- Don't spray sticking pole ends with an oily lubricant, for the same reason. Silicone is okay.
- Don't spray the tent with insect repellent; most repellents can damage the fabric or waterproof coating. One exception— repellents containing Permethrin (one brand is Permanone) are made for use on clothing and tent fabric. See page 47 for more on Permethrin.

# Tent Terminology

A quick reference for some phrases found in catalog descriptions:

**Ripstop Nylon.** Heavier threads are woven through the fabric at intervals. As the name suggests, rips are stopped by these threads.

**Hooded Windows.** The rain fly overhangs window openings; you don't have to cover the screens (and stop air circulation) in a gentle rain.

**Nylon Coil Zippers.** A continuous coil zipper, it can't bend or lose teeth or corrode like metal zippers.

**Twin-Track Door.** A doorway that has two zippers, side by side. One is for the actual fabric door, the other for the alternate screen door.

**Awning.** A fabric panel that forms a roof over and in front of the doorway to protect the tent entrance. You can cook under it if it's not raining too hard.

**Vestibule.** A small extension outside the main body of smaller tents, used to store gear.

**Roof Vent.** A square of netting sewn into the roof panel for ventilation and stargazing.

**Mesh Storage Pockets.** These are handy pockets sewn into the tent where you can keep all the small stuff you don't want to lose.

**Point Suspension Clips.** Plastic clips attach the tent canopy to an external frame.

**Storm Rings.** Rings are attached to the tent fly so you can tie it out for better support if weather is especially windy and wet.

**Seam Sealer.** Without protection, seams would be most vulnerable to leaks. Most tents are sold with a tube or jar of seam-sealing mixture, and you can also buy it separately later (see pages 138 and 139).

**Gear Loft.** A lofty name for a mesh hammock suspended from the tent ceiling. Rings are sewn into some tents for easy hang-up.

the occupants—not conducive to the tent's primary purpose of keeping campers dry. To prevent such condensation, tent roof and walls are made from a permeable (breathable) fabric that allows the moisture to pass through it so it can dissipate outside the tent. The waterproof rain fly is suspended a few inches above the tent roof so the air space between fly and roof can speed the moisture removal process.

The rain fly also protects the tent body from the sun's harmful ultraviolet rays; obviously, it is easier and less expensive to buy a new rain fly, rather than to have the entire roof panel replaced (unless someone in the family is handy with a sewing machine).

Because of their large interior volume and usual good ventilation, cabin-style tents do not have such a problem with condensation, so they do not have a separate fly. Instead, the fabric itself is waterproofed.

## Underfoot

Most tents have attached floors, made of a fabric that is tougher than the tent wall cloth, and also waterproofed. The flooring material often extends a few inches up the walls for the added protection of a waterproof tub, or bathtub, shape.

## In-between

In general, the tent takes shape in one of two ways. Either the support poles slide into sleeves/pockets sewn into the tent fabric, or the poles are connected to form the framework, and the tent fabric is clipped onto the frame—generally a much faster setup. A few designs have an interior framework that simplifies setup. Some tents are freestanding, some require guylines and ground stakes.

# MATERIALS

## Fabric

Most tents (A-frames, domes, umbrellas, and the smaller specialty tents) are made of permeable (breathable) nylon; a few are polyester (a better ultraviolet resistor). Rain flies are usually a nylon fabric waterproofed with polyurethane, or polyurethane and silicone coatings.

Tent floors may be a waterproof ripstop nylon, or polyethylene.

The exceptions to the nylon standard—cabin tents—may be made of a waterproof poplin or a polyester/cotton blend (aka polyester canvas).

Window and door screens are a fine-meshed material, usually polyester, to block no-see-ums. (If you are not familiar with these tiny biting bugs, you want to stay that way.)

Fabrics may also be treated to be mildew resistant and fire retardant.

## Poles

Most tent poles are aluminum. The better-quality metal will be described as aircraft, anodized, tempered, or "7000 series." Aluminum poles are generally considered stronger than fiberglass, but they are also heavier and more costly.

Older fiberglass poles had a tendency to break readily, but newer fiberglass/carbon fiber composites are strong and flexible. Larger tents may use steel (in a few cases, stainless steel).

The larger the diameter, the stronger the pole. Where weight is a problem, larger diameter also means a heavier pole.

With many tent designs, the separate, hollow pole sections are connected and held together with shock cord (stretchable line) for easy assembly.

# AFTER YOU BUY: A FEW DOS

When you buy a tent from a specialty outfitter, someone will usually show you how to put it up. If there isn't room in the store, they'll use the parking lot. Watch carefully; make extra notes on the instruction sheet, if necessary. (Salespeople at the family discount center would probably not be familiar with setup details, so could not help even if they were willing.)

Once you get the tent home, unpack it, lay out and check off all the parts, then set it up again, this time by yourself. Never go to a campground without having done this; it's the only way to be sure you understand the setup.

If the tent needs to have seams sealed (instructions will tell you "if" and "how"), set it up and leave it for a few hours before applying the sealer (see page 139). This way, the stitching holes will stretch as much as they can, so the holes will be filled completely.

Make up, or buy, a tent repair kit. Include some nylon repair tape for the tent and some vinyl tape for the groundcloth. If a kit isn't sold with the tent, try to get a swatch of matching fabric to use for patching.

Besides sewing supplies, take a pole repair kit: a short length of pole makes a temporary repair sleeve; slip the sleeve over the broken pole section, and tape together. Also include spare zipper sliders, some spare window mesh, a length of shock cord, duct tape, and snap-on grommets.

# SETUPS

## 2

Until the whole family is comfortable with all aspects of camping, you'll probably spend weekends at established campgrounds, where the basic scouting of the area has already been done. You'll choose to stay in a forest setting, at an inland lake or a seaside beach, or close to some other natural feature that adds to the special fun of outdoor living. Later, you'll look for less "finished" campgrounds, with fewer facilities, like those in many government parks. (You'll probably still find water and some kind of bathroom, plus a fire pit and perhaps a table.) As you venture farther afield, the list of amenities shrinks with each step away from the familiar, full-service campground. Eventually, your destination will be that perfect wilderness where all decisions are up to you.

## CHOOSING A CAMPGROUND SITE

In many campgrounds tent sites are separated from RV parking places. This is good for the tenters because their area is usually a more natural landscape, often arranged to take advantage of shade trees, pathways, or rows of shrubs that act as a windbreak and privacy shield. Sometimes, you're able to choose your preferred site: do you want to be close to the beach or the bathhouse; fish pond or gameroom; lighted walkway or lights-out forest?

Facilities vary, especially between privately owned campgrounds and government parks. Some tenting areas may still be "site only": no water or electric hookups, no extras. Others have not only water and power at each site, but also individual picnic tables and grills (or at least a fire pit). Once your site has been assigned, your main decision will be which way to face the tent door, since the actual setup spot is usually fairly obvious.

## CHOOSING A WILDERNESS CAMPSITE

### View

The classic image of a tent tucked under a sheltering tree overlooking a pristine lake with mountaintops peeking through the high clouds in the far-off distance . . . is not all bad. By all means, if you can set up a tent for such a view, *do* it. But a beautiful setting should not be the only—and perhaps not the primary—consideration, particularly since special sights will be everywhere, once you're attuned to looking for them.

### Location

As with any real estate, location comes first; for a tent site, it covers more than an address. First, look to the high ground. Camp floods are not part of the fun; even one small puddle in the wrong place can dampen your sleeping bags, your food, *and* your spirits. Besides wet gear, low land also may mean standing (stagnant) water, which in turn may bring mosquitoes.

### Space

The most basic site must have convenient spaces for the separate elements of tent(s), kitchen or

*Location, location, location. It's not always possible to find idyllic sites, but when you do, the camping is that much better.*

food preparation area, plus possibly a place for a fire. One corner of the site should be set aside as the "family room" where everyone can sit together at meals or anytime.

## Shade

If you're in the woods, you'll want the shade, to cool the air and to protect the tent fabric from too much ultraviolet; however, be wary of any low-hanging branches. While the tent canopy may clear the limbs on a calm day, a wind can push branches down as well as sideways, bringing noise and chafe you won't want.

(Trees are also handy for tying tarp guylines, hanging clothes, or suspending a food bag to discourage thievery by resident wildlife.)

## Warmth

A good site might allow the sun's rays to warm the tent in the dawn's early light, then be shaded during the daytime when the sun is high overhead. Or you might prefer late afternoon sun—for warmth during setup, dinner prep, or drying out damp clothes.

## Water

If you're in a true wilderness camping situation, you must first find a site where water is available, and then set up camp at least 200 feet *away* from the lake or stream. This ensures a water supply for you, while providing a pollution buffer for the water source.

# ARRANGING A CAMPSITE

## Site Plan

Whether your campsite is in an established campground or out in the boonies, now you must arrange it. First, assign somebody the task of noting where all movable objects (rocks, logs) are situated. If you decide to shift anything around, you'll be able to put it all back later, in order to leave the campsite the same way you found it.

As you consider your placement options, explain to the children (at least to older ones) why you're doing what you're doing. Not only will they learn the how-to of camp setup (for the time when it's their turn to arrange), but they may start to recognize the different kinds of effort that go into creating even this temporary version of "home."

## Campfire Site

If you'll be using a campfire, your floor plan will revolve around its location. Ideally, prevailing wind would carry smoke away from the front door of the tent; otherwise, you'll put the tent's ventilating

*Side-by-side tent and screen room suggest that "roughing it" is not always necessary.*

system to an unplanned test of how long it takes to air out. You also want to protect the tent from flying sparks. Try for at least 15 feet between fire and tent.

## Tent Site

Find a level spot for the tent. Don't trust your vision; lie down in the approximate spot you'll end up sleeping. It's okay if your head is slightly elevated, but definitely not your feet, and a sideways tilt is awkward and uncomfortable.

The ground underneath the tent should be as uniformly flat as possible. Pebbles and pinecones and twigs can be moved, but half-buried tree roots or rock mounds will make ordinary sleep an impossible dream.

(If the ground itself is uneven, small dips can be leveled with pine needles before pitching the tent.)

Assuming most camping will be done in the summer months, you'll probably want to pitch the tent in an appropriate position to take advantage of prevailing winds. This will give you the double benefit of cooling breezes and bug avoidance.

For those off days when you seek shelter from too much wind, try to hide behind a natural windbreak of foliage, rocks, or dunes.

## Cook Site

Set up your outdoor kitchen work station fairly close to the fire, but enough out of a main walking area so whoever is cook for the day can work easily. (If you're using a camp stove or grill, it will be part of the outdoor kitchen.)

Similarly, the eating area should be enough out of the way not to disturb the important path of plate-filling, stove-tending, fire-feeding, and other traffic.

dome tent

lean-to cooking shelter

self-contained portable toilet

fire pit

light

firewood

mat

200-foot setback (when possible)

*A canoe-in site (suggested plan).*

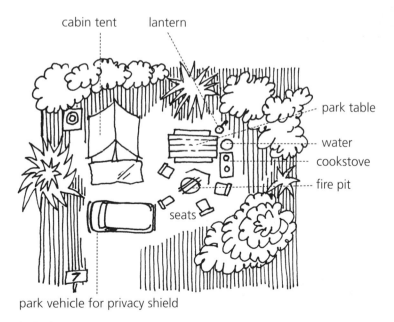

cabin tent    lantern

park table

water

cookstove

fire pit

seats

park vehicle for privacy shield

*A drive-to site (suggested plan).*

# Camping Tips

### Considerate Camping

- When signing into a campground, if you want to be close to (or far from) the bathhouse, request it. With a small child, "close to" might be a good idea. If you'd rather avoid the noise of foot traffic, "far from" is the better choice.
- Try to stay within the unmarked territorial limits of your site. Remind the children to do the same, and if you brought along your favorite friendly puppy, remember that not everyone will share your appreciation for its charming personality.
- Be sensitive to your neighbors' space; don't invade with noise or clutter.
- In wilderness areas, if you find a site where others have camped before, use that site rather than risk damaging an unused spot. (See pages 131–32 and 149–50 for more recommendations about environmental considerations of camping.)

### Careful Camping

- Walk around the campsite with the children. Look for, and point out, potential dangers such as a cliff, a cave, a soft riverbank, poison ivy.
- A line of leaning shrubs, or a lone lopsided tree, will show you the direction of the prevailing wind.
- If you camp under the tallest tree in the area, you should think about the lightning hazards: lightning can travel through tree roots, or it could side-flash if the tree were struck. The good news: occurrences of *tents* being hit by lightning are rare enough to qualify as "almost unheard of."
- When wilderness camping, current wisdom recommends 200 feet as a good distance between camp and water. The place where land and water meet is both special and sensitive. Vegetation along a shore acts as a natural filtration system, cleansing the water running into river or lake. The shallows of any body of water are breeding grounds for entire ecosystems.
- In olden camping days, campers dug shallow trenches around the tent perimeter, thereby preventing water from soaking the tent floor. Today, nobody digs; it is unnecessarily destructive.
- Avoid indentations where water can (and will) collect. Don't set the tent on mossy or other soft, spongelike surfaces; they also collect water.
- Keep a big sponge handy just inside the tent doorway. If water does get inside, you can catch it quickly.
- A layer of pine needles, or plain old leaves, makes good outdoor carpeting to cushion the tent floor and you. They can also double as a foot-wiping pad.
- A wooden pallet is an excellent shoe-scraper; the dirt falls between the slats so it can't reattach to the next pair of soles.
- A child's "play" broom is an efficient sweeper of small spaces, requiring fewer back or knee bends than a whisk broom. And you can use it to fix a tent pole.

## Rest Site

If you're in the kind of primitive wilderness place where you must set up your own toilet facilities, establish its location with *great* care. (See page 49 for particulars.)

# SETTING UP CAMP

## Union Workers

The actual setting up of your outdoor living quarters is part of the fun of camping, as you continually invent new (or adapt old) ways to accomplish familiar tasks in a back-to-basics situation. Encourage the whole family to get involved in the setup procedure. It shouldn't be too much of a hassle; children enjoy it a whole lot more than making a bed or unloading a dishwasher.

## Sub-Floor

Though most of today's tents have built-in waterproof floors, most campers put a separate tarp underneath the tent anyway. You can use a specially named "groundcloth" bought from a camping supply store, or you can use a simple polyethylene sheet such as a painter's dropcloth, found in a hardware store. (It should be thick enough so you don't destroy it with the first use; try 4 mil.)

The groundcloth-tarp should be the same shape as the tent floor, and sized slightly smaller. If the cloth were to extend out beyond the floor area, it would catch rain, and send it inboard, under the tent. Fold or trim back any extra material so the cloth can help keep the tent dry as it protects the tent floor from sticks, rocks, or other things that go lump in the night and cause holes and leaks in the floor.

(We recall not exactly fondly a canoe trip in the Everglades when the groundcloth *did* reach beyond the tent wall. The sound of dripping water, as dew hit plastic, was enough like the sound of snapping twigs to convince a half-awake camper that Albert Alligator had come to say hi.)

## Tent Raising

Each tent design will have its own set of specific setup directions, but many of the how-tos are similar.

Unpack the tent and spread the fabric out on the ground. Assemble the pole sections (most are held together with shock cord; a few of the larger tents use a light chain instead). The floor corners of some tents should be staked down before setup; others are designed to be freestanding (self-supporting), and stakes are added later only for insurance.

Next, you'll either slide the assembled poles into sleeves sewn into the body of the tent, or you'll clip the fabric onto the pole framework, raising the tent shape as you clip. Attach the rain fly last.

The tent may have fittings attached outside so you can add guylines to help keep the tent in place and in shape, especially when the wind pipes up.

# HOW TO SET UP DOME TENTS

Lay the tent on the ground. Put the shock-corded pole sections together. For the pole/sleeve design, slide the framework into the sleeves; when poles are in position and "stopped" (so they can't slide back out), the tent will take its round shape. Stake out the corners.

For the clip-on style, assemble and set up the frame. As you raise the poles into position, clip the tent fabric onto the poles.

Add the rain fly.

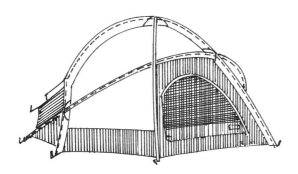

Poles slide into fabric sleeves.

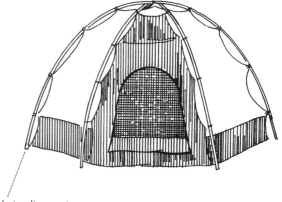

Fabric clips onto exterior frame.

*Two ways to set up a dome tent.*

# HOW TO SET UP A CABIN DOME TENT

This Remington Quick-Set Cabin Dome tent is a cross between the two tent shapes, designed to retain advantages of both. A three-minute setup time (for one person) is an appealing advantage.

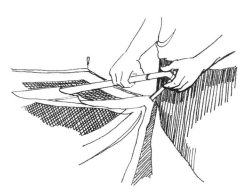

1. Lay out the tent.

2. Stake the corners.

3. Insert the ridgepole into the plastic hub affixed to the tent.

4. Insert the eave poles, which also fit into attached hubs.

5. Insert the four leg-pole sections into their corner fittings, top and bottom.

*How to set up a cabin tent. This is a Eureka! lodge tent.*

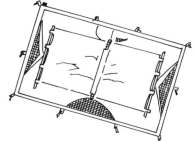

1. Lay out the tent and stake down the corners.

2. Assemble the pole sections.

3. Slide the center ridgepole and two side ridge-poles into position.

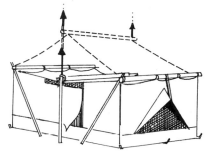

4. Attach the four diagonal poles.
5. Add the two adjustable upright poles, and extend the poles until the tent roof is taut. (It's best if two people do this, so both poles/sides go up together.)

## Tidy Tents

Just outside the tent entry, put a small plastic tarp (to keep groundwater on/in the ground) and an artificial grass pad (or rubber-tread mat or plastic carpet runner) for foot-wiping. You might use a sample carpet mat if it's ready to throw away anyway.

Keep another, smaller piece of plastic or mat next to the shoe pad, so you can leave the wiped-off shoes or boots outside the tent. The tent floor will benefit, staying cleaner longer and lasting longer, which in turn will benefit your budget.

If the tent has a covered entry extension, it will protect shoes left outside from straight-down rains. In a wind-driven downpour, you'll want to move them inside; slip them into a plastic bag for the duration, thus confining leftover twig bits and dirt plops inside the bag.

## Airborne Litter

Check the outside of the tent regularly for any residue. Remove twigs and leaves and seeds before rain or dew can cause a stain. Wash off any surprises from bird visitors as soon as possible. Do so even if you believe the folk philosophy that says such gifts bring good luck; they will not bring good anything to the tent fabric.

## Clean Sweep

Keep a small whisk broom/dust pan set near the tent doorway. (If you normally keep one in the car, move it into the tent while you're camping.) Those who forget the shoes-off rule can remove all evidence of their error quickly. (If your supermarket doesn't sell the small sweep sets, look in automotive sections of discount stores.)

## Clean Shake

Every so often, turn a freestanding tent inside out and give it a good shake, to get everything out of the corners.

# Camp Setup

You can organize setup in whatever order you choose. Once established, pack the car for the least amount of rummaging. Last in, first out.

Try the following sequence: tent, cook station, fire pit, and toilet (if necessary).

Or, food and cooking gear first, perhaps, if you plan a suppertime arrival.

### Tent Setup

Groundcloths are usually used to cover the ground area under the tent, but some campers prefer to place them over the floor inside the tent.

Since most tent floors are already waterproof, you don't need the groundcloth as a moisture barrier, and since most damage to a tent floor comes from the shoes or gear inside, an inside cover would absorb that wear before it affected the tent. It's easy enough to replace a groundcloth; not so a tent floor.

Also, when the wayward bits of bark and branches sneak inside, one good shake of the cloth is all the tent-keeping necessary.

Believers in backups could use two groundcloths; they're not a major expense.

Practice, practice, practice pitching your tent, even in the dark, because someday you'll be forced to set up after sundown, shortly after you got lost on the road that wasn't marked and your navigator couldn't find.

Don't forget to anchor a freestanding tent. Use sufficient weight inside, or stakes outside, if you don't want to see an unexpected splash of color rolling down riverbank or hillside.

When you buy a tent, pole sections may be identified by a colored dot or a stamped-on number. Make this identification more obvious with colored tape or paint, so you can readily see it by the wandering flashlight beam held by a helpful child who is more interested in site inspection.

### Pole Tips

At one time, campers carried only the cloth part of tents, and simply cut new sticks for poles each trip. In the interest of tree protection and campsite saving, those days are gone, which is why tent manufacturers strive to make poles strong but still lightweight.

- Don't try to set speed records by snapping shock-corded poles together; you may damage the pole.
- If you scratch an aluminum pole, you'll damage the anodized coating that retards corrosion.
- If one pole section is not inserted completely into the next, the pole may break.
- When disassembling poles, start at the center and work toward the ends, to keep tension as consistent as possible.
- If you should break a pole, and you didn't bring the handy pole-sleeve repair kit, slide an appropriately sized stick inside the broken section, and tape together with duct tape.
- If you can't fix a broken pole, rig a guyline and tie the tent to trees. (You always carry snap-on grommets for just such an emergency.)
- To ease assembly of sectioned tent poles, lubricate the ends lightly with silicone.

# ADD-ONS

An average-size tent should be all the shelter a family really needs to enjoy outdoor living; it provides the protected place to sleep and, when necessary, it functions as a mega-umbrella as well. But even though the idea of camping starts out with a down-sizing, back-to-nature, keep-it-simple mindset, it often becomes apparent there are many levels of acceptability within the ideal. If all family members do not share the same comfort threshold or roughing-it concept, the addition of an amenity or two could be the deciding factor in a vacation choice between outdoor family adventure, or an air-conditioned room with a view.

Fortunately, there's no end to the ways you can embellish your basic shelter. With tarps, lines, and a bit of creative thinking and tying (or stacking), you can arrange a camping setup that everybody in the family will be able to live with.

## DIVIDE TO COMPROMISE

For some people, it's especially difficult to adapt to the one-room-fits-all facet of camping life. The idea of separate rooms for separate reasons has worked so well for so long in houses, it's logical to use some of the same kinds of divisions to organize a campsite into a practical center for family fun.

### Screen Mansion

The prospect of a separate screenhouse seems excessive to the minimalist camper, but for the camper who wants guaranteed protection from burning sun or biting bugs, it becomes a necessity.

It's quite possible a screen room will be bigger than the actual tent. In spite of some half-teasing grumblings about outdoor ostentation, the campsite addition easily becomes the family room, especially once you move a picnic table inside. Here, you're shaded and bug free, enjoying the sense of outside from the relative comfort of inside.

Some of these portable porches are also fitted with roll-down panels of soft, see-through vinyl; the wind stays out and the sunshine streams in to dispel the chill of an unseasonal temperature drop.

## FRONT PORCH

Some tents are made with an attached awning— a fabric extension that shelters the tent door from sun, and provides a place to cook in a gentle rain. A few tent models are designed with an optional extension. (Eureka! makes an "Annex" for some of its tents.)

It's easy enough to put up a small tarp to shade an entrance area in front of any tent, but to keep rain out, you'd need a tarp large enough to cover the highest point of the tent; what starts as a good idea might end up with too much tarp providing not enough protection. You might prefer to use the tarp over some other section of the campsite where it will do more good.

## ROOF-OVER TARP

Freestanding canopies can be purchased, and are popular for backyards or more permanent base camp setups, but are hardly necessary for the weekend campout. A basic canopy tarp is fine— a square or rectangle of waterproof material (fabric or plastic) set up with some combination of poles,

*The screen enclosure naturally becomes the outdoor family room.*

guylines, and stakes, as a roof to cover the picnic table or any other spot you choose.

If you can tie to convenient trees, run a line between two of them. Drape the center of the tarp over the line, or tie into center grommets of the tarp. Take guylines from each corner of the tarp to other trees, or to ground stakes. Give the tarp a roof-slant so rain will roll off.

If a tree tie is not possible, set up the canopy with the poles you brought along for Plan B. You'll have a center pole that's slightly longer than the four corner poles (unless you're setting up over the table, when you may want to prop a short pole on the table). Either way, when all five poles are in position, stake out the corner poles with one or two guylines each. Position the stakes so the guyline angle holds the poles upright and the fabric taut in its rain-shedding shape.

## SIT-DOWN OPTIONS

More and more at campgrounds and parks, the once standard redwood table and bench set is being replaced by the more sturdy, but much less

rustic, cement models. We can appreciate their longevity, but they're not at all conducive to long family chats around the "kitchen table."

Folding lawn chairs are lightweight and pack fairly easily (tied on top of the car, if necessary), and they're much kinder to average body shapes. Director's chairs, with their canvas seats and backs, are

*Folding cushioned seats make comfort truly portable.*

## Campsite Comfort

- With a large enough screen-house, you can set up the food preparation area alongside the picnic table.
- Don't leave any boxed or bagged foods (like bread or cereals) in the screen kitchen over-night. The screens may not be a strong enough deterrent to the night creatures attracted by the food.
- Sectioned plates (or full trays) are great for lap dining, but they're no help at all in controlling serving portions.

- Be prepared to cushion your seating surface, whether it's earth or rock, wood or concrete. Carryable choices include a seat cushion from the car or a flotation cushion from the boat or canoe; a folded blanket, or an inflatable vinyl seat.
- Therm-a-Rest put a nonslip fabric on their mattress/chair pad, to improve sitability.
- A camp stool—either canvas stretched between wood frames or nylon mesh with aluminum tubing—is a small, very portable seat, comfortable enough for mealtimes if not for afternoon lounging.
- Camp stools also work as individual tables, vaguely reminiscent of the original TV tray.
- Use an ordinary beach umbrella as a portable porch shade, moving it around the tent doorway as sunlight shifts.
- Take the umbrella with you when you want to enjoy some quiet time with a book.

- Washable vinyl (or burnable paper) tablecloths make outdoor dining more appealing and a lot neater; you never know what forest creature was there before you.
- Buy clamps to hold the cloth to the table's edge, so wind can't unset your table (large clothespins might work, too).
- Almost all campers buy one or more of the basic blue (or green or silver) plastic tarps: they're reasonably priced and relatively strong, initially. The bad part is that when ultraviolet or use becomes too much for them, they shed tiny strands and flakes that rain everywhere.
- Pay more for good tarp fabric, and you won't have to replace it anytime soon. Choose waterproof nylon or polyester, heavy-duty canvas, cotton/poplin blend, even a UV-resistant acrylic. (If you're at all handy with a sewing machine, buy the fabric and stitch up your own tarp.)

most comfortable, but heavy and bulky to tote. Or, try the low, take-apart beach chairs that roll and pack into a compact bag.

"Sling chairs" are another popular option—their metal frames open and close much like an umbrella. Each chair comes with its own carry sack and an attached shoulder strap.

Canoe campers might prefer to use sleep pads, such as those made by Therm-a-Rest, that convert to a comfortable seat with backrest. Just fold the mattress to a right angle and insert the ends into fabric corners of the chair kit. Side straps adjust for proper tilt.

Another manufacturer, Crazy Creek, makes cushiony shaped seats, with or without the dual use of a mattress pad.

## DINING NOOK

Though some kind of picnic table is fairly standard at many campgrounds, in some parks you'll be arranging your own place to eat. If you've brought along chairs of some kind, they're all you'll need for a lap-balancing act. You may be able to find suitable stumps, logs, or rocks to use instead of chairs. (These will improve a lot with the addition of some cushioning material.) Watch the logs for signs of ants or other residents. And don't forget to put back anything you move.

## GO CHAIRLESS

Forget the chairs altogether—picnickers have done it for years. Pick a soft, shady spot with a great view; clear away the pebbles and pinecones and twigs; spread out the trusty beach blanket or yet another small tarp, and enjoy.

# TABLETOPS

If you're traveling in a van, where packing space is not so limited, a folding card table can be handy, for eating or for kitchen setup. If packing is a problem, you can get space-saving substitutes.

Folding aluminum tables (the kind with bent tubing for legs) are lightweight, work well, and store in a narrow spot. A roll-up table is another option: made of vinyl-covered wood slats, it opens out to an almost 3-foot-square table top, with aluminum legs that you screw in place.

# GO TABLELESS

Bring along a square of plywood, some leftover paneling, a couple of long boards, or any flat material that can serve as a surface to hold paper plates and serving pots. Use rocks or logs to prop it relatively level. (The spare tire, wrapped in a plastic bag and sitting flat on the ground, can be the table base.)

*Lightweight folding tables simplify mealtime.*

# OUTDOOR KITCHEN

Set up a separate kitchen area to organize cooking equipment and food preparation. The counter might be a folding table, or one big, flat rock. A lean-to tarp should be positioned overhead, to protect everything from most of the rain. The camp stove or portable grill fits here; boxes with pots, plates, paper products, and canned goods can live on top of or underneath the counter. Coolers will be on the ground, in the shade. Plan space for a bottle of drinking water, plus the portable sink and bucket for dishwashing. You might rig a clothesline for dish towels, and possibly a mesh hammock for lightweight items like bread and crackers.

At night, any food that could tempt local wildlife would be stored in the car, or in a bag hanging in a tree.

See chapter 14, "Camp Kitchen," for more tips on managing your outdoor kitchen.

# KITCHEN LEAN-TO

The kitchen cover can be rigged much the same way as the dining canopy; the difference is where the tarp hangs over the ridgeline. Instead of centering the fabric over the line, leave more tarp toward the back side so it can be tied low to create a back wall. Tie the front corners to trees or poles, or stake them down with long guylines so the downward slant is not too pronounced.

If trees are not suitably positioned for the ridgeline, use a four-pole setup in a rectangular shape, with the long side parallel to the kitchen counter. The ridgeline will be tied between the two back poles, and the rest of the setup follows the same lean-to pattern.

# HOLD-UP HELPS

Guylines give added support to tents, holding them in place and preventing escape or collapse. They also keep tarps and rain flies steady, preventing premature rips and puddle sags.

Guylines are run from tent to trees or from tent to ground. Use as many as necessary, leading them in opposite directions when it's desirable to have opposing pulls.

Attach strips of white tape or fabric to guylines so they're more visible at night. Otherwise, care-

# Handy Helps

**Guyline sliders** adjust tension.

**V-shaped stakes** help hold in sand.

**Weight** is an effective guyline anchor.

**Snap-on grommets** attach anywhere.

**Stake pullers** come to the rescue when tent stakes are really stuck.

## Knots

Camping gives you many chances to use knot knowledge. The easiest way to master line work is to do it. Take a short length of line (with ¼-inch-diameter line or larger, it will be easier to see what you're doing), look at the diagrams, and copy them as often as it takes to get the knots right. With these five knots (actually one knot, three hitches, and a bend), you can keep your camp tied up tight.

**Bowline:** Useful when you want a loop in a line. (Loop over tent stake, or tie through handle to hang anything.) Won't slip or jam; easy to untie.

**Clove hitch:** Good for fast tie-up with weight or tension on line. (Tie boat to piling or hang food bag.) Finish with half hitch for no-slip security.

**Sheet bend:** When you need a longer line than you brought, tie two together with a sheet bend. Works with different-diameter lines; easy to undo.

**Tautline hitch:** Used to adjust tension on guyline. Holds under strain, but can be easily changed when strain is released.

**Trucker's hitch:** Quick tie-down and quick-release system. Use to control tension on guyline or for car-top tie-down.

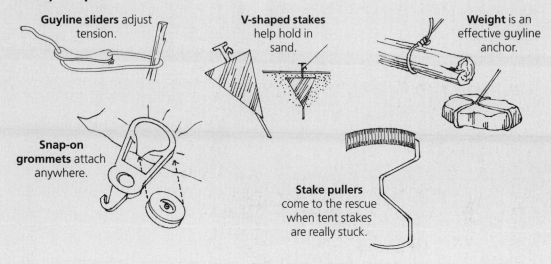

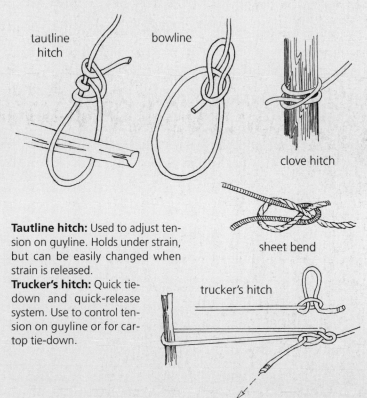

tautline hitch

bowline

clove hitch

sheet bend

trucker's hitch

*A simple tarp over the picnic table protects food and campers from sun and drizzle.*

less feet are guaranteed to find them. Or, use bright-colored line for the guy itself.

Take along extra line. For most camping applications, ⅛ inch or ³⁄₁₆ inch should work; look for parachute cord. Also be prepared with snap-on grommets or other fabric clips so you can attach extra guylines to fabric anywhere you need the line, not just where a grommet or ring might be located.

Guyline adjusters are handy. Whether slider type or loops of shock cord, they help keep fabric taut but not rip-tight.

Carry spare pegs or stakes; different designs and materials work in different ground. Ordinary plastic stakes are okay in ordinary ground; steel skewers are better in hard ground; and wider, V-shaped add-ons help in sand. When stakes won't hold no matter what you do, use rocks or logs to weigh down guylines and/or stakes to prevent them from pulling out and collapsing the tent or tarp.

# HEAT AND LIGHT

## 4

When living outside was a necessary part of long, slow travel, the campfire was purely functional, providing warmth for the travelers, fuel for cooking, and a deterrent to wild animals. As camping evolved into fun, many camping traditions began with the campfire, from hot dogs and marshmallows to songfests and ghost stories. Associations with campfires were good: the pungent smell of the woodfire, the dancing glow of its embers, the welcome circle of warmth.

The idea of camping without the traditional fire is fairly recent. Under today's green umbrella, we should think about all sides of fire. The possibility of losing control is an obvious danger, but even small, controlled fires can have an ugly side: smoke permeates tent and clothing; charred rocks stay black; soil becomes useless for years. On top of all that, fires waste wood; fallen branches should be left to decay as part of nature's cycle of renewal, returning nutrients to the soil. Nature itself will take care of any fire needed for regrowth.

On the surface, that's a hard viewpoint to refute. A simple logic suggests if we like nature, we must try to *keep* nature. If we want to see wilderness, it must stay wild.

## TO BURN OR NOT TO BURN

Whether or not you have a campfire will be partly directed by where you decide to camp. Wilderness parks may prohibit fires, at least during dry seasons, for all the understandable, good reasons. Commercial campgrounds, on the other hand, don't have entire forests to protect, and most still allow a traditional campfire;

within the confines of the existing fireplace, you can still enjoy the snap, crackle, and ghosts. And, if you should ever get lost in the wilderness, fire will be one of your most important survival tools: for heat, for signaling, for protection against animals. Everyone should know how to build a fire.

## FIRE KNOW-HOW

As countless Boy Scouts have learned, there is an art to building a good campfire, and despite a bonfire image, an overabundance of flame is not the objective. To burn well, fire needs fuel, oxygen, and heat. When wood is the fuel, it must be stacked in a way that allows air (oxygen) to circulate. The heat starts small, with the burning of paper or small twigs or other "tinder." As heat builds, larger wood pieces can be added to the fire; the goal is to accumulate a layer of glowing coals, the continuous heat supply that will keep the fire burning.

### Fire Starters

Tinder must not only burn easily, but also slowly enough to produce the heat and flame to ignite the next layer of fuel. Leaves are not very good tinder. If they're slightly green or damp, they smolder; if truly dry, they burn too quickly. Either way, they don't create the desired heat. Ideally, you'll find a bunch of tiny, dry twigs, or shreds of birchbark. Practically, you may resort to fire-starting "sticks" from the camping store. Made especially for the job, they will speed the process along.

*There is an art to building a fire, and part of it is not sending smoke into your—or your neighbor's—tent.*

Once the tinder is burning well, you add the kindling, or medium-size wood pieces, and when that layer is lit, start feeding the larger pieces of wood that will keep the fire growing.

(See page 117 for emergency fire-starting tips.)

## Firewood

At most camping places, you won't be able to gather the large pieces of wood you'll need; only so much deadwood falls in a year, and it's not enough for all the campers' fires. Never *cut* tree limbs, even from dead trees. You can often buy firewood at the campground, or you can bring

some in—probably the safer choice, as you'll be sure to bring dry, easily burned wood.

## Wilderness Fire

For those times when you are camping in a wilderness area, choose the fire's place carefully. It should be away from tree trunks or other vegetation so there's no easy way a fire could spread. If you find an established fire site, use it rather than start a new one. Enclose the fire pit with large logs, soaked with water, if necessary, so they won't burn readily. (Don't use shale or moisture-holding river rocks to line a fireplace; steam may cause them to split apart, sending rock fragments flying.) Don't build the fire any larger than you need.

If there is no established fire pit, use your own firepan and/or build the fire on top of a mound of rocks or sand. This will prevent the heat from damaging the soil.

# FIRE TYPES

If your previous experience with fire building involves charcoal grills or autumn leaves, you'll now have a chance to revert to one aspect of frontier life, with a choice of fire types. Which one you build depends partly on what you plan to do with it: warmth, light, cooking, baking, or all of the above.

## Teepee Fire

Stack same-length wood pieces in the triangular shape of a teepee, and put tinder and kindling in the center. Leave a narrow space open on the windward side of the teepee, if you need some breeze to help start the fire.

If you plan to use a cookpot hanging from a tripod, or sitting on a grill platform, the higher flames from a teepee fire are good.

rock-lined fire pit

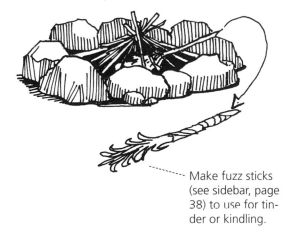

---- Make fuzz sticks (see sidebar, page 38) to use for tinder or kindling.

*The start of a good cooking fire is a well-constructed teepee shape.*

*Log cabin fire.*

## Log Cabin Fire

Start with a small teepee for the tinder and kindling, then position logs in the square shape of a cabin, making smaller squares with each stacked layer.

This fire burns fast and with a high flame, so it's not practical for slow cooking.

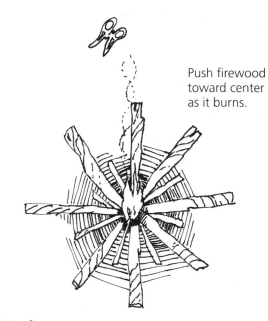

Push firewood toward center as it burns.

*Star fire.*

## Star Fire

Similar to a teepee, the star fire is a flattened version; wood lies on the ground starburst style, burning only at the end that's in the fire. As you want more flame, you simply push more sticks into the center.

With this fire, it's possible to have some control

# Fire-Building Tips

- Anytime you want to start a fire, be aware of wind direction and be considerate. It's not nice to smoke out your neighbors, and vengeance would be theirs if the wind were to shift.
- Paraffin (wax) helps start a fire. For homemade starters, soak cotton balls in melted paraffin; or fill bottle caps, or cardboard egg cartons later separated into egg cups. Put a loop of string into each wax holder for a wick.
- Other low-tech starters: slices of candles; newspapers, rolled and paraffin-coated.
- Camping suppliers sell emergency tinder kits, which include nontoxic and odorless firesticks that will light even if they've been doused in water.
- Don't use kerosene or other fuel to hurry a fire; it's not necessary, the smoke is unpleasant, and it could be dangerous. Also, if you're cooking over the fire, you may add a flavor that's not in the recipe.
- Waterproof matches can be purchased; or, make your own by dipping matches in wax. Otherwise, keep matches in a watertight jar, box, or bag. Gas-grill butane lighters also work well.

- Try to use wood that doesn't spark a lot.
- Bring a small hand-saw or axe in case you need to cut firewood into smaller pieces. (Remember, use only wood that you find on the ground.)
- Keep the firewood in the car (or propped up off the ground and covered with plastic) so it stays dry.
- Use an old charcoal grill pan for a fire pit.
- Be sure what you put into the fire is burnable. (Plastics usually melt into blobs while emitting toxic fumes. Aluminum foil just sits there.) If you guess wrong, be sure to remove the leftovers.
- If you're using flammable fuel for lantern or stove, keep it well away from the fireplace.
- With any fire shape, you can start with a triangle of wood pieces placed flat on the ground, outlining the fire space and confining the coals for a more focused heat.
- A longtime favorite fire starter is a fuzz stick. On a small, dry stick, make a bunch of notches, cutting into the wood so wood chips stand away, but are still attached to the stick. The fuzzy surface will burn quickly, with so

many spaces for air to move around.
- Don't add too much wood to a teepee fire until it gets a good start, or you may have to start all over when it stifles.
- The bright flame of a log cabin fire makes it a good signal fire. If you add some green leaves or branches to any fire, you can send real smoke signals.
- Keep a bucket (filled with water) and a shovel (to dig up dirt) near any campfire, ready to douse the fire. Never leave a campfire unattended. See "Restore the Site" on pages 134–35 for more on fire safety.

over the amount of heat you need for the type of meal you may be cooking.

# WARMING SOLUTIONS: OUTDOOR

Summer evenings can sometimes be cool, especially if you're camping in mountains. And in autumn, you *expect* brisk temperatures.

Where open fires are not permitted, you can still create some focused heat. For outdoor use, portable heaters range from the smallest charcoal grill (raised off the ground on its original tripod base) to a fireplace in the round: a large, metal bucket-like container with metal mesh sides for ember watching (assuming you won't have to carry it any distance from the car).

Camping stores sell portable outdoor propane heaters. A simple reflector mounts over a disposable propane cylinder; the reflector tilts, so you can direct heat where you want it.

The Heat Pal (looking remarkably like a bucket) holds and burns denatured alcohol and doubles as a one-pot cookstove. The heater is not pressurized; a nonflammable material inside the bucket soaks up the alcohol so it can't spill out, and it burns by a wicking process, with the alcohol coming to the surface.

# WARMING SOLUTIONS: INDOOR

Generally, heaters and tents are a dangerous combination. Fabrics may be treated to be fire-resistant, but that's not fireproof. Smaller tents don't have enough floor space to leave the required air space around the heater.

If you're at a tent site with electricity, bring a small electric heater/fan combo—and then you'll have air conditioning, too. If you decide to use any heater inside, do so very carefully. Keep it in the center of the tent to avoid melting the tent's walls, and keep fresh air circulating to avoid oxygen depletion. (Heat Pal's representative recommends you allow a minimum opening of 10 square inches for incoming air. Their heater is clean burning, but like any fire, it does use oxygen.)

If it's really chilly, the safest solution is to climb into your sleeping bags early. Everyone sleeps better when the temperature is on the cool side.

# LIGHTING UP YOUR CAMP

You don't understand "dark" until you're in the middle of a tall pine forest, miles from any city, and there's no moon at all. While the situation is great for stargazing, more basic things like walking, cooking, and changing clothes need the help of some illumination.

When you're camping where you can plug into electric power, take any small lamp from home: a gooseneck desk lamp, a clamp-on work light, individual reading lights. Even without electricity, there are a lot of choices.

*The classic camping lantern, available in single- or dual-fuel models, with single or double mantles (bulbs).*

## Classic Camp Lanterns

The classic camping lantern has been updated and upgraded and made for use with various fuels, but it still looks at least semi–old-fashioned, with its traditional shape, glass globe, and flame glow (see illustration, page 41).

The *kerosene* model is the only one that still requires preheating. This is done by pouring denatured alcohol into the burner cup and lighting it. The heating helps to vaporize the kerosene where it exits the burner. Kerosene is economical, readily available (often from gasoline stations), and, unquestionably, the safest fuel to use. A minor disadvantage is carrying the alcohol as well as the kerosene; also, some people object to the smell of kerosene, especially if it's not burning properly.

Many camping lanterns burn *Coleman camp fuel* (also described as *white gas*). Some are "dual-fuel," with ordinary unleaded gasoline as the second choice. These lanterns need no preheating or priming. Just pump up the pressure, turn the knob, and light with a match or butane lighter. Fuel for these lanterns is easily found, but highly flammable, so it must be handled and stored with care.

**39**

# Let There Be Light

- If you're using a gas lantern for light, you'll notice it puts out a fair amount of heat, too. If what you need is heat, position it low, or you won't feel the rising heat.
- If you bring a flame-operated lantern or heater inside the tent, you *must* leave an opening so fresh air can circulate. *Never* go to sleep without extinguishing the heater or light, and putting it outside.
- Pouring alcohol into the preheat cup of a kerosene lantern can get messy. You can buy a specially made plastic bottle with a curved spout, or you can try a small oilcan.
- If you choose propane, you can have stove, lantern, and heater *all* propane. Then get the proper fittings to lead them all from the same refillable bulk propane tank.
- If someone in the family suffers from icy-finger syndrome, take along a hand warmer. One such product resembles an oval-shaped, velour-covered compact. Inside, solid fuel sticks smolder, warming the case first, then the hands. (Find them at camper's supply stores.)
- When excess heat is the problem, as in a steamy Georgia summer, get a tiny battery-operated fan—maybe one for each camper—to keep some air moving around the tent at night.

- If you buy a liquid-fuel lantern, bring a funnel to ease refilling. Put a filter in it: use cheesecloth or a fine-mesh nylon to keep dirt specks out of the fuel tank.
- With pump-up gas lanterns, be sure to read and follow filling directions. The tank should *not* be filled completely with fuel; the lantern needs a fuel-air mix to burn properly. If overfilled, you'll get straight fuel at the burner, not the vapor you want.
- You can buy a perfectly sized and shaped carrying case for your somewhat fragile lantern. Or, pack it inside a plastic waste-basket wedged between the duffel bags in the car. Or, wrap the breakable globe section in bubble wrap while you're bouncing along a highway.
- Whichever lantern you choose, take along whatever spare parts or maintenance tools it might require. If it's a mantle lantern, take lots of spare mantles.
- A camping lantern is a very handy light when the power goes out at home.
- Even if you have a big lantern, take along some small candles. Sometimes you won't want the extra heat from the lantern.
- Make your own candles: First, coat the inside of a can (your candle mold) with oil (the mold release). Melt paraffin wax by putting wax blocks in a can in an

old saucepan with an inch or two of water. Meanwhile, to set a wick, weight the down end of a piece of wick in the can, tie the other end to a pencil, and lay the pencil over the top of the can (prevents wick loss). Pour in melted paraffin.
- For extra light—or a flashlight for the children—use Cyalume light sticks. They're not very bright, but they are lightweight, don't break, need no batteries or bulbs, and they're cheap.
- Popular on keychains, tiny squeeze lights can't waste battery power, can't be left on by mistake. The downside—they're not rechargeable.
- The flashlight with a "rotary turn-on" is good because it can't turn on by mistake, as a push-switch light can. But, you need two hands to do it, and that's sometimes inconvenient.
- The new, gas-filled flashlight bulbs (halogen, krypton, and xenon) give brighter light, but use more battery power. With standard filament bulbs in a flashlight, the batteries can last almost twice as long.
- Rechargeable nickel-cadmium batteries are more expensive initially than throwaway alkaline batteries, but, over their usable life span, will be the better bargain.

Next on the list of fuel options is *propane*. These lanterns can be used with disposable propane cylinders, or can be connected to a larger, refillable tank, to eliminate the problem of nonrecyclable cylinders. Familiar, convenient, and clean-burning, propane might be the lantern of choice, except that it is expensive compared to the other fuels.

And, some people are still nervous about carrying and handling pressurized tanks.

## Lantern Parts

Some lanterns have a built-in sparkmaker so you needn't bother with matches or lighter. Some have

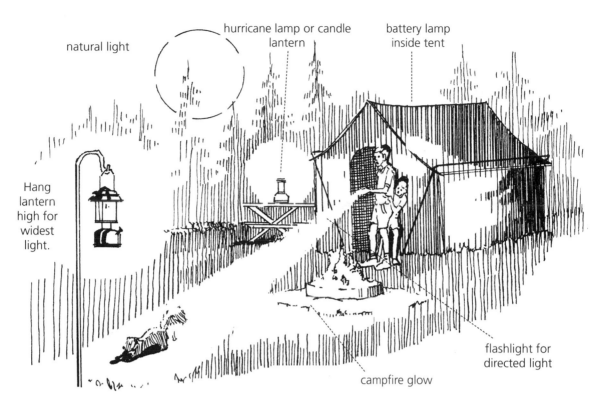

natural light

hurricane lamp or candle lantern

battery lamp inside tent

Hang lantern high for widest light.

flashlight for directed light

campfire glow

one mantle, some two. A *mantle* is the camping lantern's version of a bulb. It looks like a tiny mesh bag; it's chemically treated to spread the flame into a glowing circle of light. Eventually, the mesh burns, and the mantle disintegrates.

## Lantern Sound

Because gas lanterns all work by pressure, all emit a constant, characteristic hiss. Some people find the noise annoying, disrupting the sought-after quiet of nature. Others are able to tune out the sound, much as they might purposely ignore rock music or opera.

## High Light

To light the widest circle of your campsite, hang the lantern high. You can simply attach a wire bracket and chain hanger to a tree or post. The lantern should hang far enough off the tree trunk so heat can't hurt the bark. Or, bring along a pole/bracket. (One pole

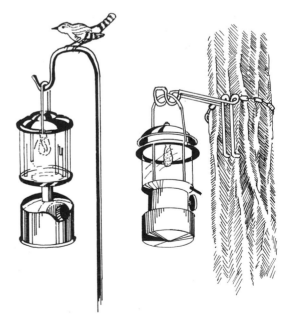

*Electrical conduit pole bent to hold lantern.*

*Bracket holds lantern away from bark.*

attaches to the top of a large propane tank—not particularly outdoorsy-looking, but practical.)

## Quiet Light

If you can live with less light, but more quiet, use a hurricane lamp instead. Small (about 10 inches high) and practical, with the charm of form-and-function, hurricane lamps burn quietly, using a wick to carry the fuel. They'll burn kerosene, lamp oil (your choice of scent), or citronella oil (an insect repellent). Few things can go wrong: fill it, lift the globe, and light. They're even reasonably priced; you can find them in basic black or red-painted metal, or a gleaming brass finish.

## Candle Lantern

You can find even smaller lanterns; some burn lamp oil, some use candles. A glass globe brightens the flame and makes the light safer for use inside the tent.

## Do-It-Yourself Candle Lights

Punch some holes in the side of a juice can (or other small can that is tall rather than squatty), and set a candle in it. Melt a bit of wax onto the can bottom to hold the candle—just like a Halloween pumpkin. Loop a wire handle into the top rim (but handle it cautiously when the candle's lit).

For better light, cut a section out of the side of a tall can and set the candle upright on the bottom of the can (see illustration below, right). For outside use, face the candle holder closed-side to the wind.

Or, use a clean can (a squat one, as used for tuna and cat food) to hold a short tub candle (see illustration below, left). Carry a couple of spares inside; in transit, cover the can holder with a plastic snap-on lid. To use, partially fill the can with sand or dirt, to hold the candle in place.

## Camp Lamps

What started with a plastic shade perched atop the rectangular flashlight/lantern battery has been refined to table lamp status. The small, portable lamps operate on D-cell batteries or the lantern battery. Some are rechargeable, and some of those recharge on either 110- or 12-volt power.

Fluorescent lanterns—battery operated or rechargeable—are efficient and double as the car emergency light.

## Hand Lamps

Flashlights have come a long way from the basic beam-pointer. They've stretched out in both length and diameter; the same flashlight can give you a focused spot or a wide angle circle of light.

*Carry extra candles inside can.*

*Cut away can side.*

They may be waterproof (some float) or PVC coated for bump and drop protection. You can find one with a clip-on handle, a stand-and-tilt base, or a wrist-tie strap. Some flashlights have two sides, with a choice of fluorescent and incandescent beams.

Basic light is all you really need. Start camping with whatever flashlights you already own; you can decide later if any features of the specialty lights might be useful to you. Soon, each camper will want his or her own light. (And some manufacturers package a family assortment for just that reason.)

## Head Lamps

One small flashlight becomes a head lamp when inserted into a loop on a headband. A real head light is much more useful than an ordinary flashlight; hands are free to put up the tent, fix dinner, or hold the map you're trying to unfold and read.

# *ANIMAL PESTS*

## 5

One advantage of an old-fashioned campfire has not changed: it's still a good deterrent to nighttime visits from wild animals, or an anytime visit from insect pests.

Of course, the animals who wander into and around popular campgrounds are not nearly as wild as their ancestors were. The resident raccoons have probably been foraging in trash cans and bins since their parents taught them how to pry off the covers. Local squirrels are practically domesticated in many campgrounds; even deer lose much of their shyness after constant exposure to people.

Despite this gradual taming (and no matter how much we might want the storybook picture of nature to be real), the truth still cautions us that these animals are not trying to be friendly; they are simply trying to take our food. Understandable though that may be, giving them "their own" food does not help them, long term; they will become dependent on (and later, demanding of) handouts, when they should be practicing the self-sufficiency that is *their* nature. Finally, wild animals can carry and transmit diseases that also affect people. Tick-related diseases and rabies are just two of the most commonly recognized.

Regardless of how pretty, cute, fluffy, or sweet a forest creature may appear, think wild, and try to send them on their own, wild way.

## ANIMAL-PROOF

Animal-proof your campsite just as you once tried to child-proof your home. When the first baby became mobile, you moved or removed whatever baby could get into or onto (or whatever might get

into baby). Do the same around the campground. Leave no food handy; remove all temptation. Put the fresh food inside the vehicle at night, not in the tent; you don't want to attract night visitors.

## CLOSE ENCOUNTER

Some curious creatures will wander close to camp anyway. Most of them (even those now semi-wild animals) will evacuate the area when you appear; probably, they sense a size difference may put them at a disadvantage. But if a little black-and-white critter is not intimidated and decides he wants to stick around, don't get too emphatic in your shooing. Let departure be his idea.

## MASKED BANDITS

If your food boxes or coolers aren't well hinged and clamped, tie them shut with a buckled utility strap, or the raccoons will be enjoying your cook-out food.

Raccoons are strong, clever, and persistent. One handy fellow lifted a cooler top and removed the snug-fitting lid of a plastic meat container before we stopped him, only by coincidental surprise. He ran off to the woods with the plastic lid in his mouth, looking like one big smile. Lesson learned.

## BEAR NECESSITIES

In most family campgrounds, you needn't worry about bears, but if you're in parkland, you may be in their territory. Check with rangers regarding bear-avoidance tactics in the area. At night, and when you leave the camp, be prepared to bag your

*Utility straps discourage masked bandits.*

## FLUFFY-TAILED FRIENDS

Squirrels and chipmunks are eager to try people food too, and while it's tempting to offer them some tiny morsel, remember they can, and sometimes do, bite the hands that feed them. While rabies is the most serious concern about squirrels, any rodent can be pesty; they'll chew their way into your food supply, given half a chance, which is why you don't leave any flimsy food packages around camp.

## BIRD BEGGARS

Discourage bird beggars, too. It may be fun, at first, to watch them catch food you toss, but the down-

food and hoist it high, out of reach of a bear standing on its hind legs.

First pack your fresh and dried food, and secure everything in one or more heavy-duty plastic bags or stuff sacks. To hang your food bag, find a usable tree limb—about 15 feet high, and extending out from the trunk far enough to prevent a small bear from crawling out to it. Tie a rock or other weight to the end of a line, so you can toss the line over the limb. That done, tie the food bag onto the line, haul it up, and tie if off to the tree trunk. Put a clove hitch (see page 33) around the tree trunk; the weight of the bag should keep the line snug, but secure the end with a half hitch so it can't slip.

You can also buy bear-resistant containers, made specifically for backcountry camping. The tight-sealing containers are designed to save your food, even if the bear gets to the container, also preventing the animals from becoming problem bears. Hopefully.

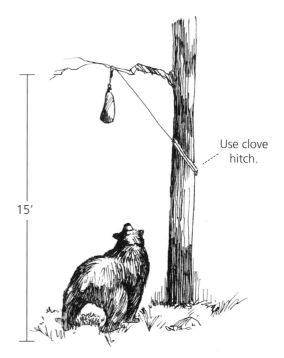

Use clove hitch.

15'

*Hang food in trees to keep it away from critters. The bigger the critter, the higher the bags should be.*

chain. Even the majority of the biting/stinging group are more often annoying than threatening. Only a few—fleas, ticks, and mosquitoes—actually carry human diseases.

Even admitting that it's their world, we still want them to stay away from the section we're usurping, at least temporarily. With luck, you'll be camped where bug habits are predictable and possible to live with: give them dawn and dusk, and you take the rest of the day. When the compromise doesn't work out quite so neatly, go to plan "bug-chase."

## Citronella

Of all the bug-chasing preparations, citronella is easiest on the humans using it—although, unfortunately, not always hard enough on the bugs. Citronella is a nonchemical repellent, made from a plant commonly called lemongrass.

You can buy citronella oil to burn in a lamp, or you can light a bunch of citronella candles. You'll also find it as an ingredient in insect repellents applied directly to skin. (See "Bug Repellents," page 75.)

## Mosquito Coils

Other burnable deterrents include mosquito coils, although these are treated with a repellent that sometimes bothers people as much as bugs. With one brand the coil sits inside a short, metal canister; holes cut into the sides allow the smoke to escape. Another holder leaves more space for smoke to exit; a fiberglass netting material over the coil keeps ashes in if the container should be knocked over.

side is they just become bigger pests. Crows, gulls, and jays are especially bad; they're not at all timid. Not only will they take your food, they may try for your water as well. (We've seen them pecking at heavy plastic water bottles and at water hoses. No luck with the bottle, but a hose might become a sprinkler.)

# BAD BAT/GOOD BAT

Bats are high on almost everyone's list of least favorite woodland dwellers. Like many mammals, they *can* carry rabies. On the good side, they consume great quantities of mosquitoes. They're not exactly camp pests; they don't go out of their way to come to a lighted, active campsite. But you may find them if you go for a moonlight stroll. Their flight is distinctive—a fast dive or swoop rather than a wing flap. It's often repeated: their sonar is amazingly accurate. Trust it.

# BUG CHASERS

On the basis of numbers and pester-ability, the smallest pests win. Biting bugs—whether flying or crawling—seem the constant enemy. But while the campsite is the first line of defense, don't be overly aggressive about bug-killing. Try to remember that most bugs are good: they pollinate flowers and food plants, and are the first link in many a food

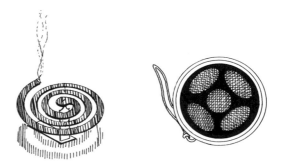

Left: *Metal stand holds coil; put aluminum foil (or foil pie plate) underneath to catch ashes.* Right: *Metal can holds coil; fiberglass mesh keeps ashes confined.*

# Natural Encounters

### Skunks

Lucky for us (and the other animals who share the same habitat), skunks are not aggressive. Lucky for them, they're equipped with a powerful protective mechanism. Skunks don't have to rely on evasive action or excess speed. They can stand their ground and guard their territory with the mere threat of a spray attack. Ordinarily, a worried skunk will send warnings before using his unique weapon. He may arch his back like a cat, move backwards, and sound a low growl. When the tail lifts, he's out of warning signals.

If a surprise encounter with a skunk results in your worst camping nightmare, two old stand-by solutions may help with cleanup— tomato juice or a vinegar/water mix of about 1 to 10.

### Bears

If you're deep in bear country, you may be advised to cook in one place, then camp in another, so no food or food smell is at camp. Always clean fish well away from the campsite, and dispose of fish scraps properly. In coastal areas or at a fast-moving river, toss into the water. Otherwise, if you have a hot fire, burn them *completely*, or pack out (well wrapped). Don't leave the aluminum foil used to cook dinner on the grill overnight. The barbecue sauce smells as good to the animals as it did to you.

Bag anything that might smell interesting; even toothpaste could be mistaken for candy. Keep a separate bag for the empty cans you'll be packing out. (Bonus bag benefit: while bagging and hanging food is primarily associated with bears, this precaution also keeps your food from becoming the prime objective of an ant trail.)

If you should actually see a bear watching your campsite, make loud noises and hope he'll leave the crazy human alone.

### Porcupines

Like skunks, porcupines don't worry too much about enemies; most animals cannot get past the porcupine's outer armor of quills. Porcupines spend most of their time in the trees that are their food source, munching happily on leaves and buds and twigs and bark—hardly a diet to fight over. If threatened by an animal unfamiliar with its defenses, the porcupine turns tail-to, and with one swat, sends out a bunch of barbed quills. The porcupine cannot literally throw the quills, though that's a popular belief. Once the quills touch something, the barbed ends quickly attach themselves, delivering a painful lesson to the would-be attacker.

### Bugs

During the day, try setting a bug attractor at the outskirts of the campsite. Suggestions for the bug lunch include pancake syrup, sugar water, or honey; corn cob, watermelon rind, apple core; anything fresh enough to appeal to a bug. Leave the bug plate about 10 or 12 feet away from *your* plates. At night, fit a cover of nylon mesh netting over each cot or sleeping bag as a second line of defense against mosquitoes.

Other tips:
- Be kind to dragonflies, which can consume great numbers of the local mosquito population.
- Wish for a comparable natural predator for no-see-ums, one with an insatiable appetite and unlimited intake capability. (You may not see an invasion of these tiny flies, but you'll know they're around when you feel countless tiny bites on your scalp, eyebrows, arms, ears, wherever.)
- Keep a fly swatter visible. Often, the sight of this ominous weapon convinces flies to keep their distance. If it works, buy bright Day-Glo–colored swatters.
- Best of all bug chasers, choose a campsite that will benefit from good breezes so the little lightweights aren't able to hang out in your territory.

The portable smoke-makers are actually more practical than a campfire for bug control. You can move *them* upwind, instead of moving yourself downwind.

## Permethrin

An insect repellent in a water-based formula, Permethrin is EPA approved for use on clothing and tent fabric. One application will be effective for two weeks, even if it rains on the tent (or you wash the clothes).

## Personal Defense

Chapter 10, "Camper Cautions" (pages 74–75), suggests ways to keep bugs off yourself.

# *BACK TENT*

## 6

Almost all campgrounds, whether privately owned or government parkland, have some kind of bathroom, ranging from simple pit toilets (a newer version of the original outhouse) to full-facility bathhouses with flush toilets and both hot and cold running water.

When you're camping in wilderness, things are not so familiar. You can join the rest of the outdoor world and go natural, or take a more civilized alternative and carry along any of a number of flush toilet substitutes.

## MOVABLE PLUMBING

*Portable toilet* describes a surprising number of transportable toilet substitutes, starting with a cedar bucket (or junque shop chamber pot) and progressing to a real Porta Potti.

A trademark of the Thetford Company, the name Porta Potti is so perfectly descriptive, it is used as a generic, much like a certain famous facial tissue.

For those who've never used a portable toilet, it's a square-shaped plastic box, divided into two sections (top and bottom) clamped together. Open the hinged top lid, and behold, a tiny toilet bowl. Between the inner bowl and the outer square is a space that holds water for rinsing. A pumping mechanism brings out some of the water to rinse the bowl after use. To flush, you pull a handle which opens the bottom of the bowl, allowing waste to fall into the bottom-section holding tank.

When the tank is full, you simply disconnect it and take it to a place of proper disposal, such as a campground toilet, or the "dump station," a des-

ignated hole in the ground which connects to the campground sewage treatment system.

A more basic version of a portable toilet resembles a plastic hassock, and holds a bucket-type toilet discreetly inside. Another style is an actual bucket, outfitted with the familiar seat and lid.

An experienced backcountry camper recommends using a 5-gallon paint bucket with snap-on lid. Line the bucket with a plastic bag. After use, double-bag the contents, seal, and get rid of the bag. (Keep spare bags handy under the liner bag.)

Flush-Me-Not goes a step further. With this product, a plastic bag again lines the toilet or bucket, but after using it, you pour in a powdered absorbent (with neutralizer and deodorant) which gels the toilet's contents. Close the bag with a twist tie, and throw it away. (For space considerations, a folding toilet-seat-on-legs can be easily carried and used with the bags.)

The point is, you needn't worry too much about toilets. "Bring your own" is apparently big business.

## TOILET TREATMENT

As you might guess, except for the disposable-bag types, these toilets require some kind of immediate treatment, and camping store shelves are lined with choices.

If you're like most outdoor folks, you'll look for the green lines: biodegradable; environmentally safe; natural enzyme; no harsh chemicals; no perfume; no dye.

The holding tank treatments are available as liquid or powder, or in tablet form. The newer non-

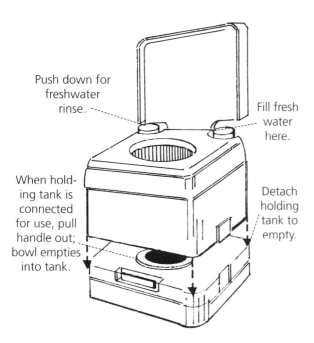

Push down for
freshwater
rinse.

Fill fresh
water
here.

When hold-
ing tank is
connected
for use, pull
handle out;
bowl empties
into tank.

Detach
holding
tank to
empty.

*Portable toilet.*

chemical additives are coincidentally better for the
eventual sewage facility, with fewer mystery ingredients. They also have less of the penetrating odor
of earlier chemical treatments.

# TOILET TISSUE

Tissue is specially made for use in portable toilets; it
disintegrates readily, to reduce the risk of clogging
holding tank or plumbing. It is also specially priced.
If you don't have the camper's special, use the
thinnest one-ply paper you can buy. Best of all is a
one-ply tissue made from recycled paper; it starts
to disintegrate almost on contact with water.

# OUTDOOR TOILETS

For wilderness camping, you'll need an out-tent, a
place for a bathroom when there is no real bathroom. (Check local practices and regulations when
you camp in wilderness areas.) When setting up
camp, locate the latrine area downwind of the
main camp and as far away as practical. If you're
not using a holding-tank toilet, remember the distance between "rest room" and stream or other
water source is now recommended to be 200 feet.

Having established a suitable place, you can use
one of the portable toilets already described, or
consider this option.

## Flowerpot Pot

Take along an extra-large plastic flowerpot and
base. Before you leave home, cut out the bottom
of the pot, leaving no sharp edges—this is your
toilet seat. At your wilderness bathroom, dig a
small pit about 6 to 8 inches deep and turn the
flowerpot upside down over it. Use the base for a
lid. Each time you use the flowerpot, cover the
waste with a scoop of dirt. When leaving the
campsite, refill the hole completely.

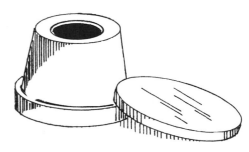

*Cut hole in bottom of plastic flowerpot; place
upside down over poop pit. Use inverted flowerpot
base as lid.*

# Toilet Tips

- Even in a campground with full bathroom facilities, any of the small portable toilets would be handy in the tent, for small children and for adults who want to avoid the midnight stroll to the bathhouse, especially in the rain. If you don't want the pot in the tent at night, put it in the car or van, or set it outside next to some bushes. Darkness will give you privacy, and you'll still save the hike to the bathroom.
- Take disposable toilet seat covers, in case the campground facility hasn't been properly cleaned, or for on-the-road pit stops.
- If you buy holding tank treatment in liquid form, carry and store it very carefully to avoid a messy spill. Tablets (or individual packets of premeasured powder) are easy to use.

- Along the Appalachian Trail, hikers are able to use a privy; waste is then composted, in one of the more practical examples of recycling.
- If the plastic-bag-in-a-bucket is the toilet, wilderness campers don't urinate in it. Urine does not do significant damage to soil or plants, but common sense should tell campers to go as far away from camp as is practical, for their own sake as much as for those who follow.
- Take a hint from one of nature's neatest beasties: Use a cat hole. The most basic of outdoor toilets is the one-use hole you dig (use a small trowel or camp shovel) and refill immediately after use. Cover waste with ashes, dirt, moss, pine needles; this keeps down odor and germs and keeps away flies. As for toilet paper, cats don't worry about it, but people should. Never bury it, and avoid burning it, which can be a fire hazard; it's best to bag it (in another zip-top bag) and pack it out. Natural alternatives include sphagnum moss or soft green leaves.
- Store toilet paper in a covered plastic container or a zip-top bag so it can't be rained on.
- Save end-of-rolls from home, so each person carries his own

small roll of paper from tent to toilet.
- In some places, river rafters must carry out all waste, a challenge to backcountry toilet technology. (Spare holding tanks do provide one answer.) With that for comparison, the cat-hole system seems almost genteel.
- Much has been written about outdoor toilet tools and techniques, one popular favorite being *How to Shit in the Woods*, 2nd edition, by Kathleen Meyer (Ten Speed Press, 1994). While such books may not belong with the greater literature of the Western world, humor might help a reluctant camper accept a less-than-perfect solution to an unavoidable problem.

Any collapsible toilet seat—or a jury-rigged seat on a frame—can be used over the wilderness pit, or with the disposable bags.

Young children are often fascinated by these new options in the world of toilet training and will want to use them more often than necessary. A few may be nervous about a toilet that has no reassuring flush; this attitude is the greater problem. In either case, introduce the portable toilets at home, long before the first camping trip and when you *have* an acceptable alternative.

Children may not be the only ones to experience initial problems with a changing toilet scene. Attitude adjustment is easy to suggest, less easy to accomplish, but creating a sense of privacy makes a good start. Extra effort in setting up a wilderness bathroom should not be considered a waste of time.

# PRIVACY SHELTER

Set up a vertical rectangular enclosure of polyethylene for a true back tent. Or, let a slightly smaller camping shower room (see page 71) serve double duty.

It's also possible that natural foliage may provide a privacy screen, with no help from a separate portable room.

Or, string a few lines in a triangle or square space around the site, and clip on rain ponchos, big garbage bags, or beach towels on any exposed side of the "rest room."

# WILDERNESS CLEANLINESS

In lieu of a bathroom sink, put some liquid hand soap or a soap-on-a-rope near the outdoor toilet. Keep a gallon bottle filled with water for rinsing. (An empty liquid laundry detergent bottle is much sturdier than an ordinary water bottle.)

Moist towelettes are good hand cleaners, too.

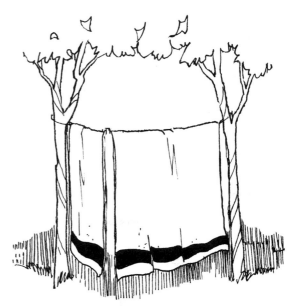

*Use beach towels (or large plastic garbage bags held in place with clothespins) as privacy screen.*

# THE CAMPERS

# CAMP BEDS

## 7

Nothing is fun if you haven't slept well. No matter how much you may want to enjoy the pleasures of sun rising, wood fire smoking, coffee steaming, and bacon sizzling, you won't even recognize them if you're still in sleep mode. All the jokes about grumpy-in-the-morning can't change the way you feel.

If you're going to like camping, you must do everything possible to ensure good sleep every night. Luckily, it's not hard to do. The first thing you should notice about sleeping out is that the combination of outside air and outdoor activity often leads to instant sleep; as soon as head hits pillow, you're off to slumberland. Then it's up to the combination of underbody cushioning and overbody covering to ensure your continued rest until early light starts the next adventure-filled day.

## SLEEP PLAN

The shape of your tent floor will have the biggest influence on the family's sleeping arrangement. It may be a sardine line-up or a modified spoke plan; follow-the-hex-walls, or three-in-a-row and one crossways. Whatever the eventual positioning, be sure nobody's leaning against a wall. In most tents, the side walls are made of a breathable fabric; if there's any moisture on the outside of the tent wall, you might wick it through to the inside by touching the wall. (Also, when you roll up the sleeping bags in the morning to organize the tent as day room, be sure no sleeping bags or duffels touch the side walls.)

## CAMP COTS

They're not meant to compare with box springs or inner springs, but a camp cot will keep you off the ground. Cots will work only in a tent with sufficient headroom and near-vertical walls.

As basic as they seem, even cots require choices. First check the way the cot is made. Metal supports at head and foot can be uncomfortable if you're tall (long) enough to touch them, or if you're not cushioned well. Some cots are made without these end bars. If at all possible, try before you buy; at least, take a survey of other campers who've used cots.

Check the way the cot stands, and imagine how the supports might affect a nylon tent floor. (Bent, rounded tubing is easiest on the tent, but other styles could be cushioned to protect the tent fabric.)

Most fold in half for carrying and packing; one rolls up into a lumpy tube shape. Compare materials: look for sturdy, mildew-resistant fabrics, and consider the convenience of removable covers.

## GROUND CUSHIONS

Many campers would rather sleep on the ground than try to stay balanced on a cot frame, especially sleepers who like to sprawl or move around a lot. Canoeists, of course, don't even have the cot option—no room in the canoe. Fortunately, nobody has to sleep directly on the ground; campers can pad their sleeping area in different ways. Basically,

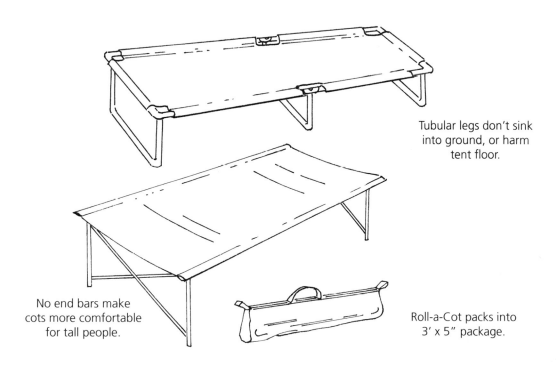

Tubular legs don't sink into ground, or harm tent floor.

No end bars make cots more comfortable for tall people.

Roll-a-Cot packs into 3' x 5" package.

*Camp cots.*

these divide into three categories: air mattresses, foam pads, and the more recent addition to sleep tech, the self-inflating foam mattress.

## Air Mattresses

Most air mattresses are variations on two styles: the full-length, tubular-shaped *I-beam* construction, or the non-chambered fake button-quilt look in a square-cornered, flat mattress. They're made in an assortment of materials, but the rubberized canvas seems most favored; even though it may be heavier, it has a softer touch. (The heavier weight also means heavier-duty, as it lasts longer.)

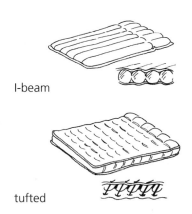

I-beam

tufted

*Air mattresses ensure the most comfort for the least weight and packing space.*

Air mattresses sound like a perfect solution. They carry small and light; when filled, they provide a large, fairly thick mat, which should be the most comfortable, but some people have trouble. Here, too, a lot depends on the way you sleep. If you usually sleep flat on your back or your stomach, a single-size air mattress will be fine. If you like to curl up or stretch out, you'll probably find some parts of your body will over-reach the boundary of the mattress and be suspended with no support beneath them. At best, you'll find a workable compromise (usurping portions of your neighbor's mattress); at worst, you'll roll off the edge of the mattress from time to time. (One tubular mat has separate valves so you can make the outer tubes more firm than the inner, to help prevent a roll-off.)

## Foam Pads

Instead of an air mattress for cushioning, you may choose to sleep on a foam pad. A full-length pad is naturally most comfortable, but it makes a bigger bundle to pack and carry, so many campers settle for a three-quarter length. A thickness of ⅜ inch is the minimum, and it is truly minimal for comfort. Buy pads as thick as you can pack; the ground pad not only provides cushioning, but insulation as well.

Closed-cell foam is a "rigid" foam, a dense material that cushions well and doesn't absorb water. Since they don't compress, closed-cell pads are bulkier than open-cell, when comparing equal foam thickness.

Open-cell is the spongy foam; a thicker pad may be more comfortable, but since it can absorb water, it requires more care. (Some pads are fabric-covered, to help keep the foam dry.)

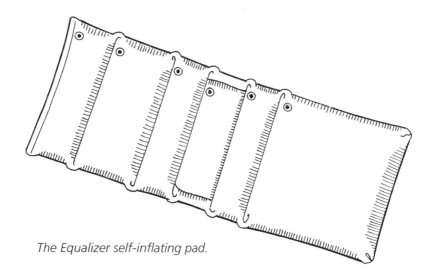

*The Equalizer self-inflating pad.*

## Self-inflating Pads

Self-inflating foam pads cushion with both foam and air. The Equalizer camping mattress uses separate chambers, so you can adjust the amount of air for different parts of the body. Three of the chambers are connected, so air flows through; three are independent.

Therm-a-Rest is a popular mattress for good reason. Its open-cell foam compresses to a smaller package. To inflate, open the air valve, and air flows in. (You may need to top off with your breath, especially when the pad is new or has spent time rolled up.) To deflate, open the valve again, this time to release air, and roll up the pad, pushing air out as you go. When it's rolled tight, close the valve. (You may have to sit or kneel on the pad to get the air started out.)

Therm-a-Rests are made in full- and three-quarter length; two can be connected for a double bed.

To prolong the life of the mattress, it's important to store it properly (see page 140).

# SLEEPING BAGS

Bags are most practical for camp bedding. They're cozy for sleeping, and even young children can roll them up and out of the way come daylight.

A lot of sleeping bag features are built-in for cold-weather camping, designed to keep sleepers warm in near-freezing temperatures. Summertime campers don't need all the extra detailing and super-tech materials; they may want to be covered, but not cocooned. Families may already own sleeping bags for the kids, from bring-your-own-bed slumber parties. Adults can buy a similar, lightweight basic bag from a discount or department store, and take along a few old wool blankets to pile on top if the weather report calls for chilly nights.

As you expand territory and season, you may want to invest in a serious sleeping bag, and since they are an investment, multiplied by how many family members camp, they require some prior study.

Bags are made in two basic shapes, each with a modified version.

• *Rectangular* is the roomiest, so you have the most freedom of movement. They sleep the coldest, but that's not a problem for summer campers.

• *Semi-rectangular* or *barrel* shape tapers at the feet and a bit at shoulders; with less space inside, it warms up faster than a rectangular bag.

• Shaped and tapered, a *mummy bag* has the least space to heat; made for cold-weather camping, it also has a head-covering hood. If you move around a lot when you sleep, you won't like the confinement of a mummy bag.

# Pillow Talk

### Cots

- One kind of metal-framed cot is designed with one end raised. If your pillow is less than fluffy, you'll still be able to sleep with your head elevated.
- A 2-inch foam pad covers another cot. This is probably the closest you'll get to a real bed. (It could double as the spare bed for house guests.)
- Most camp cots are about 6 feet long by 24 to 28 inches wide, but one design measures 84 inches by 31 inches. Those extra inches can make a big difference in sleepability, even if you're not overly tall.
- You can buy bunk cots: one pair can be set up as a double-layer bunk, or as two separate singles. These may be handy to own if one of your children sometimes brings along a cousin or friend.

### Air Mattresses and Sleep Pads

- Repair patches are often included with air mattresses, a reminder to keep tent floors on smooth ground.
- You can buy single or double air mattresses with separate inflation valves for their built-in pillows. Not only can you control the amount of air in each section, but the pillow doesn't shift every time you do.
- Small hand or foot pumps are available, but the bellows-type foot pump is the easiest to use, and it gives somebody good leg exercise besides.
- A bicycle tire pump would work, too.
- Never inflate a mattress with compressed air; it's too much pressure for the fabric and seams.

- If you have a station wagon or a van, get a station wagon pad to use for one double mattress.
- To provide a better surface to help hold the sleeping bag on a sleep pad, some pads have a ribbed pattern; others use egg-crate foam or rely on a non-slip fabric over the pad material.
- If you have arthritis, use a good, thick sleep pad. Your hips will thank you.
- If you don't have a manufacturer's repair kit for your sleep pad, take along some self-adhesive nylon repair tape, or seam sealer, to use on pinholes.
- When your Therm-a-Rest pad is new, you might need to blow into it a few times to help speed inflation. Later, it will be more willing to self-inflate.

### Sleeping Bags

- If it's a cold night, sleep on your next-day clothes so they'll be warm in the morning.
- Practical campers appreciate the efficiency of a sleeping bag that tucks a foam mattress into its underside. (The bottom half of the bag doesn't keep you warm anyway, since the insulation is compressed by your weight.)

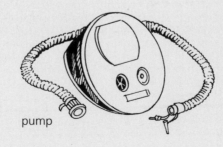

pump

- If you want connectable sleeping bags, remember that rectangular (including barrel-shaped) bags will pair as top and bottom sections, but with mummy bags you'll need a right-side zipper and a left-side zipper.
- If your bag is sackless, buy or make one, or use webbed utility straps to hold the bag when it's rolled.
- Sleeping bags carry temperature ratings ranging from 30°F or 40°F for warm-weather bags to minus 45°F for true winter expedition conditions.
- Buy a bag suited to the climate you are most likely to find most of the time you camp; then use extra clothes or extra blankets for the few unseasonal chills.
- Down is the warmest, lightest, fluffiest, most compactible, most durable of all sleeping bag insulations. Its lone disadvantage: if it gets wet, it's useless; it is no longer warm, and it does not dry quickly. It's also the most expensive fill, and for the average camper, it's too hot.
- A specialty sleeping bag is designed just for women. It's narrow at the shoulders, wider at the hip; it has more insulation at torso and feet area. Of course, it's a mummy bag.
  - Buy or make a sheet liner (percale or flannel) for your sleeping bags. The bags will stay cleaner longer, and on a hot night the liner will be all the sleeping bag you want.
  - A neat, efficient child's sleeping bag can grow.

## Pillow Talk (continued)

Two zip-in fabric extensions stretch the bag from 39 inches to 55 inches. From Tough Traveler KidSystems (800-GO TOUGH).

- Make a temporary "sleeping pen" for baby by arranging duffels around a triangular or square space. Baby sleeps in the middle, cushioned on any side a nighttime rollover might send him.
- If one child gets chilled easily, arrange sleeping spots so the child is positioned between two less-cold-prone bodies, whether parents or siblings.
- Buy a different color sleeping bag for each person, for instant identification.

- A hammock is usually associated with hot nights: where else can you get so much exposure? But the relaxing sway might be equally welcome on a cool night. Just pop your sleeping bag in the hammock and curl up.
- The hammock doubles as a swing for baby. Put one over-tired youngster into the hammock; give the natural swinging action a little boost, and soon you'll have a happy little snorer.
- If your sleeping bags are average lightweights, keep blankets in the car for the few times you might need them. All-wool

are the most dependable for warmth.
- Wool blankets in army khaki or navy gray make great camping blankets: warm and tough.
- If you take real pillows, put two or three cases on them for extra protection. (The outer pillowcase can pack homeward-bound laundry.)
- Stuff an extra sweater, towel, pile jacket, or flannel shirt into the sleeping bag's stuff sack and use it for a pillow.

---

- A *modified mummy* shape tries to ease the claustrophobia without sacrificing too much heat-keeping ability.

"*Flex*" bags from Sierra Designs offer another option. They incorporate a series of elastic bands that "hug" the bag to your body, allowing you to sleep in any position—side, back, or tummy—comfortably.

## Double-Bagging

Family campers will probably get the basic rectangular bags. Two of the same model bag can zip together into a double-bed bag; this also works with barrel-shaped bags. You can use two of the same length, or put a longer bag on the bottom.

Most sleeping bags are made for an average-size adult, but if you're above average in height,

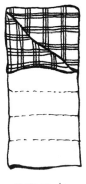
rectangular

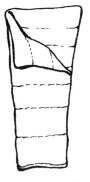
semi-rectangular

mummy

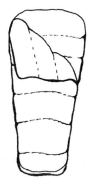
modified mummy

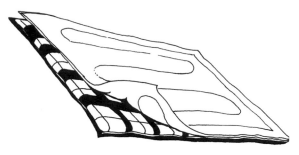

*Zip two bags together for a double bed.*

look for extra-long. If you're otherwise oversized, or simply like more room to move, look for extra-wide or jumbo (and ignore the label). A few bags are made in children's sizes, too.

## Temperature Ratings

Tags on sleeping bags give numbered ratings that are more significant to mountain and expedition hikers than to summer campers. Since the numbers are not based on any industry standard, they can only be considered as a basis for comparison on the most general level.

## Materials

Shell fabrics and insulating materials (usually called *fill*) could fill their own book. The combination water-resistant/breathable shell fabric is not something the summer camper needs, nor is down fill, even if it is the warmest insulation. For practical reasons, get a sleeping bag with an easy-care fabric and synthetic insulation, and throw it into a washing machine when need be. (See pages 128–29 for more about gear for backcountry treks and off-season camping, and pages 138–40 for additional care and storage tips.)

Before you buy your investment-grade sleeping bag, you may wonder about some other descriptive terms:

*Loft* describes how insulation fluffs and retains the air pockets that do the actual insulating.

*Fill power* is a way to compare insulation, and refers to down's resiliency, or *loft*. When you

see "550 fill," that's the number of cubic inches an ounce of down takes up; an ounce of that particular down fluffs to 550 cubic inches. Synthetic insulations use the same comparison.

*Baffles* are interior fabric walls that prevent insulation from shifting about.

*Offset quilting* is the way two layers of quilting are sewn together, so the seams are not in line (cold air could sneak through an uninsulated seam, and warmed air could sneak out).

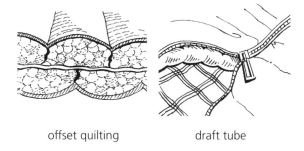

offset quilting　　　　draft tube

*Draft tube* is a fabric tube filled with insulation, covering the zipper on a sleeping bag, to prevent heat loss through the zipper.

## Special Bags

One practical solution to varied-season camping is a bag with different amounts of insulating material on each side. When it's cold outside, sleep with the fuller, loftier side on top. When it's warmer, sleep with the lighter side on top. (With any bag, the underside doesn't do much to keep you warm, because the would-be insulating air spaces are compressed by your weight. The top side always has the warming function.)

## Custom Bags

At least two companies have found a niche selling everything the competent home sewer needs to make sleeping bags for the entire family (and also whatever clothing items require the special fabrics not found in the corner fabric store). Patterns, fabrics, insulation, fasteners, even cutting tools can all be mail-ordered from Quest Outfitters (800-359-6931) or Rain Shed (503-753-8900).

*Two children can share a small tent and a sleeping bag.*

# FOR CHILDREN ONLY

Babies sleep like babies in a portable playpen, which also serves as a useful safe haven during the daytime. Later, they'll use a sleeping bag and mat of their own.

For safety, let a small child sleep between two adults, or at least on the side of the tent opposite the entrance, so there's no chance of an attempted moonlight stroll without your being alerted by the crawl-over.

Little children can share a grown-up's sleeping bag; just unzip it and use it as an under-and-over comforter. (If you wait till they're exhausted to put them to "bag," they'll be less inclined to have a giggle-fest playing footsie.)

"Middle-aged" children can share an adult-width bag, a good sleep setup when they are also sharing a separate small tent.

Children's sleeping bags are made in a couple of lengths. These are fine hand-downs, but if no second child is waiting, they're outgrown too soon.

To bring an adult bag down to size, roll up the unused foot portion, clamping it shut with a long bag clip or giant clothespins. (Or, fold it underneath for extra protection from the ground.) You may lose some of the insulating property due to compressing the bag where it rolls; if feet are cold, you can always toss a small blanket over the end of the bag.

# HAMMOCK HAVEN

A hammock is hardly required camp gear, but it can be such a good extra, for night sleeping, day napping, and best of all, mind clearing.

A hang-anywhere bed lets you loaf in the nicest places. Beachfront is a personal favorite; the cooling touch of a steady sea breeze, the lullaby of endless waves, and the gentle swing of your private cocoon puts your world on hold—*and* gives you something to call on for future stress management.

A cotton woven hammock is probably the most comfortable, though it will mildew and rot eventually. You can also find them in nylon or polyester twine, or a solid canvas fabric. Wooden spreader bars at the ends of some hammocks hold the shape, but they must be well padded or they destroy the feeling of unhampered freedom.

You could forget the tent if you sleep in a jungle hammock. With mesh net sides, a fabric top, and a cotton canvas floor, you have a self-contained, functional, elevated shelter with all the fun of a hammock.

*Hang hammock so bottom is close enough to ground for easy entry.*

# BASIC BED

If you don't own sleeping bags, you needn't purchase them for your first camping trips; just take as many blankets as you think you might need, and pile them on. The only problem with this plan is that if you're sensitive to the blanket fabric, you'll need sheets to separate you from the blanket, and now you're bringing more items than you might want to tote around. Still, it works.

## Starter Sleeping Bag

Make your own starter sleeping bag with a light cotton blanket or flannel sheet (double-bed size). Safety-pin or sew the lightweight cover to a heavier blanket (also double-bed size); then lie down on one half and pull the other half over you. This is only temporary; use big needles and big stitches, and it goes fast.

## Pillow Tech

Some people simply cannot sleep without a real pillow. If you usually bring pillows in the car, they don't seem like too much of an extra when you move them into the tent.

You may be able to substitute a small foam-filled pillow for the real thing. Or, try a poly-filled pillow form from the fabric store. Last choice would be an inflatable.

# CAMP CLOTHES

## 8

For ordinary camping, most people don't need to buy any special camping clothes, with the possible exception of rainwear. Just go through your closet and dresser drawers; pull out all the sportswear that's starting to get faded or thin, but isn't quite ready for the work clothes bin, and you'll probably have an adequate camping wardrobe.

## LAYERED LOOK

The concept of layering clothes as a way to create insulating air spaces is a fine idea for serious hikers, who also need to pay close attention to fabrics' wicking or absorbent capabilities. For average campers, layering is more like be-prepared packing: when it gets cold, you add layers; when it's warm, remove them (up to a point).

Before leaving home, you'll be aware of, and pack for, the expected temperature and weather conditions; an extra sweater or a sleeveless T-shirt will help get you through the unseasonable whims of mother nature. Be sure to double-check weather conditions at the place you're going as well as the place you live. Three hundred miles can make a big difference in a weather pattern, and when those miles are due north, you may want to concentrate on the sweater section of your add-ons. (Our first camping trip to Quetico Provincial Park, just across the Minnesota border, was in late August. We dressed for a warm, south Michigan summer, and found 32°F nights.) A similar temperature change will be apparent with higher elevation, or if you head to the coast from an inland home.

## TOPS

T-shirts seem to be everyone's favorite—perhaps as much for their messages as for their versatility as clothing. The basic cotton T-shirt is a practical choice for hot-weather wear; it absorbs perspiration, and the dampness helps keep you cool.

Together, T's and sweats remain the camping standards: long sleeves, short sleeves, or no sleeves; in different weights to wear separately or to layer. Plus, they roll up for easy packing and wrinklefree wearing. Just remember that cotton fabrics are a liability in cool weather when wet—either from perspiration or damp weather.

## BOTTOMS

In choosing what kind of long pants to take, go for the tougher fabrics: denim jeans or heavy twills that won't be bothered by tree snags or a brush with a rock. They'll help protect your skin, and they'll make life more difficult for any biting bugs.

Here's an exception to the don't-buy-new rule: Army fatigue pants (or copies, like carpenter's or painter's pants) are very practical around a campsite; with so many pockets and loops to file things, they save you steps. You can carry a pocket knife, folding scissors, plastic bags for collecting shells, a candy bar, a compass, Band-Aids . . . important stuff.

If you happen to own the kind of shorts that look like abbreviated fatigue-type pants, bring those, for all the same reasons. On a summer day, when you're not traipsing through the bush, shorts are more comfortable and much cooler than long pants.

*Pants with lots of pockets are very handy.*

For the children, bring plenty of loose-fitting short sets or playsuits in the toughest fabrics available.

If you're camping where a typical summer day's activity includes jumping in and out of a swimming pool or lake, you'll probably spend the day in your swimsuits, solving everybody's what-to-wear questions.

## OUTSIDE

A light cotton jacket, or possibly just a long-sleeved flannel shirt, will be all the outerwear you need most summer nights. For spring and fall camping, think layers again.

Wool, in whatever form, is still best for warmth; it continues to warm you even after absorbing moisture (in case the rain gets to you before you get to the tent). A wool-blend shirt or sweater is good, a double-back jac-shirt even better—an extra layer of wool covers shoulders and upper back, just where you often need the extra warmth. Fleece cover-ups are also warm, and don't have the problem of absorbing moisture. They're less itchy, more comfortable than wool.

If it's particularly breezy, a simple windbreaker (or pullover-style *anorak*) fits over the last shirt. Not only does a windbreaker help hold in your body heat, but it provides some water resistance in a drizzle. (Get one with a hood hidden in the collar.)

A longer jacket (*cagoule*, in camping supply catalogs) is better than the standard just-below-the-waist windbreaker length. It covers the lower back, where you might feel a chill wind, especially when you're sitting down. The longer style usually has a few extra pockets, too—always handy at camp.

## HATS AND GLOVES

Campers need hats mostly for sun protection. Straw hats are airy and cool; white hats reflect more heat. An extra-long-billed cap or visor shades the face for more hours of the day: as the sun comes from lower angles, the cap's shadow still covers your nose.

Bring light-colored, lightweight, fun hats for the children, something they'll like enough to actually wear.

*On a chilly day, a lightweight fleece jacket provides warmth and comfort.*

# Clothing Tips

- *Wickable* fabrics (Capilene, polypropylene, acrylic) take moisture away from the skin so it evaporates outside the fabric. This makes them the ideal choice for hiking in cool weather.
- *Absorbent* fabrics hold moisture; in summer heat, an absorbent cotton T-shirt will dry slowly, keeping you cool.
- Wear denim coveralls for really good "overall" protection. Even wearing suspenders with jeans will keep more of you covered more of the time by keeping pants up, shirts in.
- Light-colored clothes are good for tick-spotting.
- On a cool night, much of your body heat will escape if your head is not covered. A sailor's wool watch cap packs small, warms well. A hooded sweatshirt protects against the night chill, and if it's a cold sleeping night, you can wear it to bed (use a pullover style; zippers get cold). Night caps may look silly in old movies, but they were popular for a reason. Cover your head and neck, and your body stays a lot warmer.
- Most campers don't bother with pajamas. A loose-fitting sweatshirt and pants are comfortable; if it's cold, thermal wear is a chic alternative.
- Even in warm weather, long-sleeved shirts may be more practical, for the extra protection against sun or bugs.
- If someone in the family is supersensitive to sun, you may want to look at the clothing made by Sun Precautions. The fabric itself has an SPF of 30; it's made to block more than 97 percent

of ultraviolet radiation—both UVA and UVB. Call 800-882-7860 or go to their Web site (www.sunprecautions.com).
- Since you may someday need to actually wear four or five layers of clothes, be sure the outer layer is big enough to fit over the others. When you do buy new jackets, buy big.
- A wide-brimmed canvas (or straw) hat will help keep you cool and sun-proofed. (A chin strap assures that it will stay on, even in wind.) Also, a visor is nice (if you aren't balding!).
- A bandanna looks very woodsy. Use it as a headband/sweatband; tie it around your neck, or wear it like a hat; make a pouch to carry wild berries (never mind the stain); use it for a bandage or a sling.
- A large plastic garbage bag becomes a usable poncho; cut a hole in the bottom and put it over your head.
- Buy rain gear from a store that specializes in work clothes. It's sturdy and adequate for camping use. And, it's reasonably priced.
- Renew a water-repellent finish

on nylon jackets, tarps, duffels, and packs with spray-on (or wash-in) products from Nikwax or DuPont.
- If you have cold feet, wear slipper-socks to bed. At night, don't wear the same socks you've worn all day, even if they seem dry; a touch of moisture means cold toes! Roomy footgear allows thicker socks and better circulation, hence warmer feet.
- Wool socks stay warm when wet, a necessity for canoe campers and anyone prone to cold feet.
- If you plan to do much hiking, take some good sport socks. The wicking ability of synthetic fabrics to carry moisture away from skin, coupled with extra cushioning, helps prevent the friction that causes blisters. Wool socks also cushion well.
- Many campers like a pair of rugged sport sandals, too.

## Packing

- If each child takes care of packing his or her own duffel, the overall packing—at home and at camp—will be less of a chore. Double-checking is still better than doing the whole job.
- If a youngster still has a security blanket or a favorite sleep toy, put it on the master list.
- Make a contest out of tidiness. Of course, the prize must be worthy of the effort expended, or there will be no effort at all. Or, have the children pretend they're in the army, and you're the drill instructor. (This works only if they're old enough to have seen the right movies, which they probably aren't and haven't.)

*A longer jacket is practical at camp, keeping the lower back warm.*

Summer campers may use gloves more for working than for warmth—for example, to wear when cutting wood. (For the chilly evenings of off-season camping, mittens keep hands warmer than gloves.)

# RAIN GEAR

If you *want* to buy good rain gear (and canoe campers should), you can find a lot of choices in waterproof/breathable fabrics, but they're not inexpensive. None are perfect protectors, but many people prefer them to the old soak-or-sweat cover-ups. Gore-Tex is the most often recommended but other fabrics are also waterproof/breathable.

Those who can handle a sewing machine might consider buying fabrics and patterns from the same sources that sell materials for do-it-yourself sleeping bags (see "Custom Bags," page 60).

An inexpensive poncho made of rubber, vinyl, or rubberized fabric is probably all car campers need for the amount of time spent outside in the rain.

*A poncho packs small but provides good protection.*

(After all, "rain" is why you have a waterproof tent.) The poncho is a versatile item around camp. It can be a temporary rain fly or tarp, or a privacy shield for the shower or portable toilet; use it for a groundcloth if you forgot to bring the real one.

# SHOES

Choose your shoes according to what you plan to do. For basic camping, wear your most broken-in sneakers or moccasins or work shoes; grubby is not a problem. Sturdier walking shoes are fine for ordinary day hikes from the campsite; if you already own them, bring along your lightweight hiking boots or hybrid hikers/sneakers. If you're camped near a river or other shore, you may want water shoes to grip slippery rocks.

No matter which day shoes you take, you shouldn't wear them inside the tent at night. For that, bring a pair of soft leather moccasins; they'll tuck into a small corner of the duffel, and your feet will be ever grateful.

*Even if hiking is limited to short day hikes or mini-mountain scaling, shoes should be suitable for the terrain.*

# DUFFEL TALK

If you don't own any duffels, you can find matched sets of sporty designer models, or stick with simple carry-bags; soft luggage is sold to fit every budget.

Army duffels are super-strong, but probably bigger than you need, unless you want to pack family-style. They're not too practical for weekend camping, either—because they're end-loading, you must empty everything out to get to items on the opposite end. When you live out of a duffel, a full, top-opening zipper style is better.

Nylon (or similar synthetic) bags are lightweight, but still durable. A Velcro-closing flap overlapping the zipper contributes to a bag's longevity.

Better-quality bags will have more features, and they're good features, even if they're not necessary. A padded strap is a big help if you're toting for any distance. Separate zippered compartments are very handy and help you stay organized. (Think birthday gifts for the children. Maybe they'll like a bag done in an arty version of camouflage.)

If each person has their own duffel bag, a different color from the rest, packing is easier all around. Also, it is immediately obvious who needs lessons in duffel neatness.

# PACK TALK

If you already own suitably sized backpacks, use them for packing, perhaps along with some smaller duffels. Toting gear into a campsite is easier when the load is strapped to your back; you're better balanced, and your hands are free to do or hold other things. (This is especially important on a canoe trip with a lot of portages.)

Most campers take dayhikes away from camp, and a daypack is the ideal way to carry jacket, extra socks, water, lunch, snacks. Children can use their book pack as a daypack. Fanny packs are commonly used everywhere for everyday essentials.

# CAMPER CLEANUPS

## 9

For many campers, the shower-a-day routine stays at home. You're living in the bush, you're sleeping in your clothes—how clean do you have to be? Men may choose not to shave for the duration, and children, who often consider bath time wasted time, are delighted with their newfound freedom to be a little grubby without guilt.

This is not to suggest campers can't stay clean; the key word is *choice*. If you want to shower every day or three times a day, you can. If not, you don't. (With exceptions allowed when water is scarce or tent-mates declare ultimatums.)

## CAMPGROUND BATHHOUSE

Sometimes, the shower facilities at a particular campground will influence your showering decision. If the bathhouse is cleaned and aired regularly, and has unlimited free hot water and no waiting, then daily showering is a pleasure. If the maintenance person is missing, the heater doesn't work, or there's one shower stall for 40 campers, then showering moves down the list of priorities.

Fortunately, most commercial campgrounds do maintain good, clean bathhouses. Many owner/managers are campers themselves; they know how one bad experience means no return trips, not to mention the damage done by the well-traveled word-of-mouth network.

Regardless of how clean a shower floor looks, it's good insurance to wear flip-flops or some kind of shower shoes, to avoid picking up any undesirable conditions like plantar warts. (Nobody can be expected to disinfect the shower after every use.) Be sure the soles of your shower shoes don't get slippery when wet.

Camper supply catalogs also sell a foot mat made of redwood or cedar strips. The platform keeps your feet off the shower room floor (or off the ground, if you're wilderness showering), and the nonskid surface keeps you from slipping.

## BATH ACCESSORIES

Camp towels usually come out of the home linen closet, chosen by the "oldest and thinnest" process of elimination. If possible, assign a different color towel to each person, so there's no question of whose towel accidentally found its way into the puddle of mud outside the bathhouse.

If you're stuck with the same color towels, you can still separate them with an identifying mark on the label, or a few loops of bright-colored thread sewn into a corner.

If your home towel supply is too new to provide camping towels for everyone, check out a special lightweight made-for-travel Packtowl. The fabric (not cotton) absorbs much more water than a standard towel. Then, you simply wring it out, getting rid of most of the water, and it's usable again right away.

Each person should also have their own shower kit. You can buy individual cushioned nylon travel kits, monogrammed or otherwise differentiated. Or, women can use a small purse, retired from primary use because of scratches or worn spots. Children can use a similarly scarred former book bag or lunch box. Anybody can use a small canvas tote bag.

A larger tote bag keeps clothing, towel, and shower kit at hand, hopefully hanging within reaching distance of the shower. Unfortunately,

# Cleanup Tips

- When you shower in the campground bathhouse, take a vinyl-covered clothes hanger, a loop of shock cord with hooks at each end, or a piece of flat-iron bent to fit over a door or shower rod. This way, you'll be able to hang up your tote bag filled with shower needs.

- When the bathhouse is not spiffy-clean, carry a small spritz bottle of disinfectant soap and a few paper towels, to wipe down the sink area before using it.

- If no sign is posted, ask the campground manager what time of day the showers are closed for cleaning, so you won't be surprised or disappointed.

- Recycle old screw-top prescription bottles to carry shampoo in a shower kit.

- A daily scrub of face and hands uses only a small amount of warmed water to help you feel clean and refreshed.

- Look for liquid soap made specially for outdoor use. Sun-Shower Soap is one brand—it's concentrated, biodegradable, and lathers in fresh or salt water. (Check marine stores if you don't find it at the camper's supply.)

- If you're not sure of the water quality at the campground sink—or if you just don't like the taste of iron or sulfur—keep a small bottle of "good" water to use when brushing your teeth. A 16- or 20-ounce plastic soda bottle holds enough water, and cannot splinter into thousands of glass slivers.

- If you forgot the toothpaste, use salt.

- Don't forget the dental floss; in camp, it does double duty as emergency thread or string.

- Men can leave the shaving cream at home. Shampoo is a good substitute, and if you use an unscented brand, you'll attract fewer bugs.

- Cover any water bottle with anything black, and leave it in

the sun to warm water, for any purpose.

- Keep moist towelettes at camp, to clean hands of campground grime before cooking, or to clean faces of barbecue sauce after eating. They provide a quick, refreshing scrub anytime.

- If you're at a camp with good shower facilities, you'll be able to rinse facecloths thoroughly to use them again. If you don't have a lot of water, don't bother with the facecloth; the one-time use isn't worth packing one in and out.

- Bugs seem to like scented soaps, shampoos, and toiletries. Instead of using your usual deodorant, try unscented varieties, or as the Arm & Hammer people suggest, "dust underarms with baking soda, as needed, to feel fresh all day."

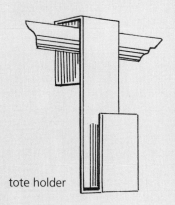

tote holder

suitably placed hooks or even nails are not always found.

Collect a bunch of little sample-size bottles for shampoo, liquid hand soap, or lotions, so everybody can carry what they need in their own bag. Then when things get lost, no loud accusations are possible—in a perfect family.

Soap stays neat in a bar-sized, covered plastic box. Holes in the bottom of the Soap Caddy allow water to drain out, so soap doesn't turn to unusable mush. An attached line hangs the Caddy from showerhead or faucet. Keep a small shampoo bottle and a razor stored safely in the shower, in a second Soap Caddy.

# WILDERNESS BATH HUT

Weekend wilderness campers seldom worry about showering. They may use a lot of moist towelettes and face cleaning pads, but a full shower is hardly a necessity in a back-to-nature experience. When you set up camp for a week or two, however, part of the setup should include a way to bathe. Whatever method you choose, don't use the nearby lake or stream for a bathtub. No soap degrades instantly.

## SunShower

Camping and boating catalogs will show the popular portable shower kit called SunShower. Pour water into the black, heavy-duty plastic bag, leave it out in the sun till the water's warm, then hang the bag so gravity feeds the sprayer hose attached to the bottom of the bag. You control water flow with a clip on the hose. (Hurry the warming with stove-heated water.)

At first, you'll have to consciously practice conserving the water, but once you get accustomed to using it, you'll find the original 2½-gallon size is adequate for a one-person shower and shampoo. (Larger sizes are available, for longer showers or more than one.) A secondary advantage: The SunShower takes little packing space; when empty, it packs as flat as any plastic bag.

## People Sprayer

For car campers with enough space, another portable shower setup uses a 2-gallon garden bug sprayer. Either fill it partway with cool water and add heated water, or wrap a black plastic garbage bag around the filled container and leave it in the sun for a few hours. Either way, when the water's

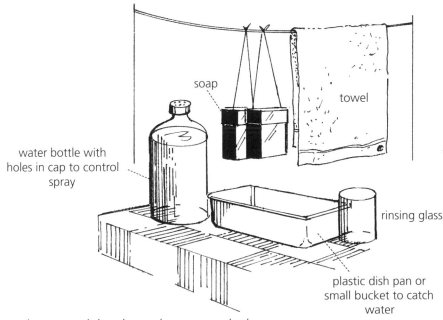

soap

towel

water bottle with holes in cap to control spray

rinsing glass

plastic dish pan or small bucket to catch water

*Set up a place to wash hands or take a sponge bath.*

gravity-fed "SunShower"

foot mat

*Portable shower enclosure.*

a sprayer. Pour as needed. (A garden spray can is already equipped with a spray tip. Just fill and use.)

## Shower Curtain

Whatever washing aid you choose, you'll probably prefer to use it with some privacy. You can buy a portable shower room; or you can make a simple arrangement using guylines to hang plastic bags or beach towels in strategic, view-blocking places.

## Dry Shower

When camping in places where water is hard to get or unavailable, you can still wash your hair and your body with products that don't need to be rinsed away. Appropriately called "No Rinse," both shampoo and body-bath make washing suds using only a small amount of water. You wash with a cloth or sponge, but after washing, you don't rinse; just towel yourself dry. It may sound strange, but it worked for NASA astronauts as well as for more down-to-earth expeditionists. Find it in camping catalogs, or call the company for information: 800-223-9348.

You'll find other specialty products, too, like liquid soaps that work in hot or cold water, fresh or salt; or dry shampoos that you brush in, then brush dirt out.

# CLOTHES CARE

Take along a small laundry bag. Nylon is good, mesh may be better for damp things—less opportunity for mildew to invade.

You'll want a clothesline (or a roll-in-or-out laundry reel) for swimsuits, beach towels, bath towels, dish towels, and everything else that needs air drying.

Rig a clothesline inside the tent, as high as possible. If things are still damp at dusk, you can move them inside to prevent a resoaking from dew.

If it becomes necessary or desirable to wash a few clothes, use the campground self-service laundry, or hand wash a few items. Put water and a splash of laundry or dish soap and the dirty clothes in a bucket or a large zip-top bag. Set them in the sun to soak for a few hours; then slosh a bit, rinse a lot, and hang to dry.

warm, pump up the pressure and shower away. (If you replace the attached spray hose with a kitchen sink sprayer hose, you'll get a better water flow.)

## Primitive Shower

Punch holes in the bottom of a bucket. Hang it overhead. Another person pours water (preferably warmed) into the bucket as you stand underneath. (Success here depends on the second person getting up high enough to pour.)

Or, you can make a sponge-bath or hand-wash station. Fill a large, screw-top bottle with water, and cut holes in the lid so pouring water works like

# CAMPER CAUTIONS

Just when you're starting to think about all the good times you can have camping, here come the warnings. But this chapter shouldn't put a damper on the anticipated fun. Consider it a collective reminder; when you're aware of potential trouble spots, you can prepare to deal with them.

Camping isn't so very different from picnicking in your backyard. You'll be staying outside longer, and more outdoor problems may arise, but most of them are typical and familiar. The insect world has no boundaries. Too much sun can be a problem everywhere, and so-called "poison plants" can grow almost anywhere. The exceptions—scorpions and certain spiders and snakes—are a concern only in some areas.

## TO THE CAMPSITE

For the car campers: If anyone's prone to motion sickness, prevention starts the day before you leave. Eat a light supper—no fried foods, no hot spices. Pack the car with boxes of pretzels and crackers, vanilla wafers and ginger snaps—all easily digestible settlers for unsettled stomachs. Favored drinks are apple juice, ginger ale, or flavored seltzers. (Ginger itself may be a nausea preventive; get pills from a health food store.) Sitting in the front seat also lessens the queasy feeling for some people; it's better to watch the scenery than the interior of the car.

## AT THE CAMPSITE

When the tent is up, everyone should go on a walkabout to look for anything that could be regarded as a hazard, especially after dark. Note the location of sharp rocks, large roots, messy mud, or problem plants like poison ivy and nettles.

Remind the children of safe-camping rules: Don't trip on the guylines. Don't get too close to the campfire. If you're camping near a river or lake, never go near the water alone, and always wear the flotation vest in boat or canoe. If you see a snake or an animal, leave it alone: no feeding, no chasing, no bothering.

## SUN DAMAGE CONTROL

It's no secret excess sun is bad for your skin. Despite persistent denial by sun worshipers, "tan" is a signal that your skin is calling for help.

### Sunburn Stoppers

You could hide from the sun all day, but that defeats your purpose of being outdoors, and, fortunately, isn't necessary. Sunburn prevention, however, is a priority. Wear light-colored clothes, to reflect rather than absorb the sun's rays. Long-sleeved shirts and long pants cover more skin, but are not always a complete solution: you can burn right through clothing. Wear hats or visors with long brims or bills, to shade your face. Watch out for reflected sun—rays bouncing back from a boat deck, water surface, sand, even a cement patio.

### Sunscreens

Where suntan lotions once encouraged a tan, sunscreen lotions now try to prevent it. Sunscreens are rated with SPF (sun protection factor) numbers that tell you how long you can stay in the sun without burning. If you'd normally burn in 10 minutes, and you apply a sunscreen with an SPF of 30, you should be protected for 300 minutes (10 minutes multiplied by 30 SPF).

Sunscreens don't have a cumulative effect; two coats of SPF 10 won't be a 20. They're waterproof for a time, but excessive perspiration can take away some of the protection. For ordinary activity, reapply every two hours; more often when swimming or exercising.

## Sunblock

A sunblock will stop the sun's rays, preventing both UVA and UVB from reaching your skin. Sunblocks use either zinc oxide (the original opaque white nose protector) or titanium dioxide (newer blocks may be translucent or skin-colored).

## Child Protectors

Children's skin is extra sensitive. Unfortunately, sunscreens should not be used on infants. Keep them out of direct sun; shade with umbrellas, canopies, sunbonnets. With older children, start the sunscreen habit as early as the pediatrician recommends.

## Burn Soothers

Despite your precautions, someone may get burned. Be prepared with aloe vera gel or an aloe-based ointment; give aspirin or other pain reliever to ease the burning, and lots of water to prevent dehydration. Cool compresses will soothe the skin temporarily; and, of course, further exposure to the sun should be avoided.

# HEAT DAMAGE CONTROL

Sun can do more than burn your skin. On a hot day, anybody can overexert, prompting excessive perspiration that could result in heat exhaustion.

*A hat provides sun protection for your face and neck.*

The symptoms are extreme thirst, heavy sweating, headache, dizziness, possibly nausea. Anyone with all or some of those symptoms should sit quietly in the shade, drink water, and hope the feelings subside. If they don't, the problem might be the more serious heat stroke; and that could be fatal, if the condition is ignored.

Initially, many symptoms are similar; the big difference is that skin is usually hot and dry. Breathing may be alternately deep and shallow, pulse alternately weak and strong. Muscles may twitch;

the person may become disoriented. If you can't get to a doctor immediately, splash the person repeatedly with water, to cool them off as quickly as possible. Give water to drink (assuming they're conscious).

To prevent both conditions: When it's hot outside, be sure to drink lots of water, or "sports" drinks like Gatorade. Avoid alcohol and caffeine. Keep cool with ice, or by fanning yourself. Plan activities for cooler times of day. Stay in the shade as much as possible.

# PROBLEM PLANTS

Everybody knows they should not touch poison ivy, but there ends the common knowledge. People expect to see a climbing or creeping vine, but it also grows as a shrub. Deer and other animals eat it, so it's not universally "poisonous." While some people aren't sensitive to the plant, most are; the standard reaction is an itching rash that must usually run its irritating course.

Poison oak and sumac raise the same kind of lumps as the ivy. Try not to scratch them; it will only spread the rash.

# BUG DAMAGE CONTROL

From a human perspective, bugs have no redeeming qualities. Mosquitoes are pesky and persistent. No-see-ums are sneakier because you almost cannot see them. Blackflies are just plain mean: one bite and you bleed. Chiggers literally get under your skin.

## Bite Discouragers

Denim, canvas, and twill jackets and pants are too tough for small biters. Light colors seem less attractive to bugs than dark. Cloth shirts are better than knits (the stingers will find those tiny holes). Wear heavy socks and leather shoes. Rubber bands around sleeves and pant legs will discourage up-bound crawlers; or you could tuck pant legs into the tops of heavy socks.

You can try an Original Bug Shirt, a hooded pullover style made of cotton so densely woven, bugs can't bite through it. Mesh inserts help keep you cool (800-998-9096). Or you can buy an entire outfit—jacket, pants, and hat—made of bug-deterring mesh.

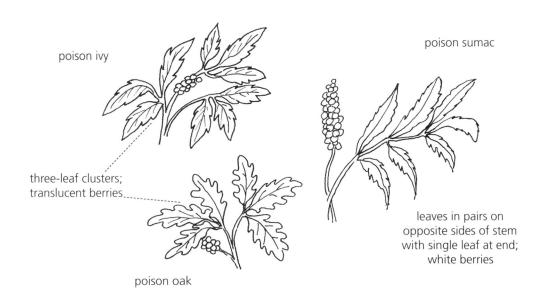

poison ivy

three-leaf clusters; translucent berries

poison oak

poison sumac

leaves in pairs on opposite sides of stem with single leaf at end; white berries

Fragrances attract bugs, so don't use anything scented.

## Bug Repellents

There are many bug-repellent products, but the basic repelling ingredients in most are the same. Citronella is easiest on you, but less effective on some bugs. DEET-based repellents are the most effective on the worst bugs. (DEET is the easy name for N, N-diethyl-meta-toluamide.) Even though DEET may damage varnish and polyester fabric, the number of side effects people report is extremely small. Read label warnings, and use only as necessary. If you don't like using chemicals on your skin, you can spray your clothing and tent with a repellent containing Permethrin (Permanone is one).

For years, Avon's Skin-So-Soft skin moisturizer saw secondary use as an effective repellent against mosquitoes, no-see-ums, and (some say) blackflies. Now bottled and labeled for anti-bug use, the familiar scent was—and still is—found on the most unlikely wearers.

## Bite Treatment

Despite the best repellents, be prepared for bite treatment. After Bite is a popular product; its ammonia-in-mineral-oil formula neutralizes the effect of a bite, and its pen-type applicator is neat. Many other products can ease the itch: Bactine, Solarcaine, first-aid creams, calamine lotion, or home remedies like vinegar or baking soda.

Chigger bites might need special treatment. Chiggers burrow under your skin and raise itchy welts, often around a waistband or wherever clothes are snug. Some people claim a coating of clear nail polish suffocates them.

# STINGERS

Camp areas have their share of stinging insects, too: bees, wasps, and hornets are everywhere. Really, they're good guys who go about their pollinating business until we get in their way.

If you get stung, you may find the actual stinger stays in your skin after the bug has gone. First, scrape the area with a dull knife, to ease the stinger out without releasing any more venom. Then, remove the stinger with tweezers; wash, and apply ice and something to ease the stinging (any bug-bite treatment, or alcohol). Benadryl—pill or ointment—may help.

Any stinging thing can trigger an allergic response in sensitive people. If a person develops hives, headache, nausea or vomiting, wheezing, dizziness or fainting, or swollen face or tongue, get to medical help quickly. People who know they're allergic carry a special treatment kit wherever they travel.

# ARACHNOPHOBIA

The dislike of spiders is not new. Judging by the number of insects they dispatch, spiders should enjoy more favored status. Only a few have bites which might be harmful to people, and while bites are not exactly common, it's better to recognize those that might be a threat, so you can ignore all the others.

The black widow can be recognized by a red/orange hourglass shape on the underside of the abdomen. A bite *is* nasty and can cause local pain, sweating, and intense abdominal pain; but almost all victims recover.

A bite from the brown recluse or "violin" spider produces severe pain and local swelling, sometimes weeks after the bite; there may be chills, nausea, or fever. In the area where the poison was injected, tissue may be destroyed.

At one time, the name *tarantula* conjured a terrible threat (or a terrible movie plot). Now, people keep them for pets, also regarded as terrible by others in the household. While tarantulas *can* bite, they seldom do, and the bite is not significantly poisonous.

As with any bite, wash and disinfect. For severe pain, apply ice or a cold compress, and see a doctor.

# TICK-PHOBIA

Ticks are arachnids, too, but fear of ticks is more justified: they can carry human disease. One of these is *Rocky Mountain spotted fever,* carried by the ordinary dog tick. If you've been bitten by a tick, and develop a rash along with headache and high fever, see a doctor. Untreated, the disease can be fatal.

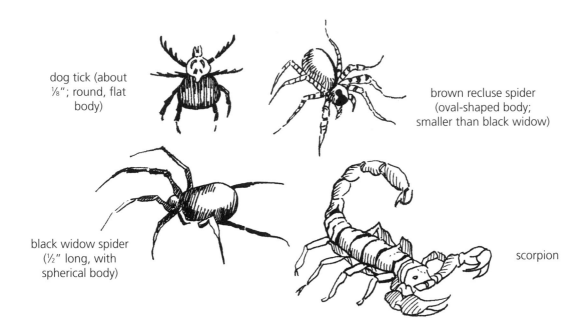

dog tick (about ⅛"; round, flat body)

brown recluse spider (oval-shaped body; smaller than black widow)

black widow spider (½" long, with spherical body)

scorpion

*Lyme disease* is spread by the bite of the tiny tick commonly associated with deer, but it is also found along with field mice or other mammals. "Tiny" means about the size of a fat pencil point; they're hard to spot on clothes or skin, though sometimes you feel the tickle of tiny legs as they crawl. Their bite usually (not always) shows as a circular red spot. Diagnosed early, Lyme disease can be cured with oral antibiotics. Untreated, it can produce many problems, including neurologic or cardiac abnormalities, joint inflammation, and more. Once considered a threat only in the northeastern U.S., Lyme disease is now found all over the country.

The newest tick disease to worry about is *ehrlichiosis*. Originally identified in the Midwest, it is now believed to be found wherever the Lyme tick lives. Curable with tetracycline, its nonspecific symptoms make diagnosis difficult. Always tell the doctor if you've been in tick territory; otherwise, you may be treated (or not) for flu.

To remove a tick: Even if you catch a tick in mid-bite, you can't brush it off; they burrow partway into the skin. Use tweezers and try to remove the tick with a steady tug. (You'll need the smallest needle-nosed tweezers you have to remove a deer tick.) Many people think a tick will relax its grip if touched with alcohol, kerosene, or nail polish.

Official recommendations either ignore the practice, or deny that it helps. Once the tick is out, wash and disinfect the bite. Save the tick, to show the doctor if the bite becomes infected.

Vaccines are now availabe to help ward off Lyme disease in people and dogs. However, they are not 100 percent effective and are somewhat controversial. Discuss the advisability of a vaccination with your health care provider.

## SCORPION SCARE

Scorpions are related to ticks and spiders, but are unique in their biting mechanism: scorpions inject venom through a stinger in the tail. Besides causing severe pain, a sting may bring nausea, abdominal pain, and possibly shock or convulsions—all good reasons to shake out sleeping bags, shoes, and clothes when camped where scorpions live. Also, be careful if you pick up a rock to pound in a tent peg.

## SNAKE ID

It's hard to find people who *don't* dislike snakes—though, given a choice between them and rats, many choose the snake, however grudgingly.

Snakes don't sit around waiting to attack people. Bites usually occur because the snake was startled. Only four North American snakes are poisonous. Three—rattlesnakes, cottonmouths (water moccasins), and copperheads—are pit vipers: head shaped like an arrowhead, with an indentation, or pit, between eye and nostril on each side. Fourth is the coral snake, a relative of the cobra, with a blunt head and round eyes. Other snakes have similar markings, but on corals, the color order is yellow, red, yellow, black (and repeat). Remember: "Red on yellow, kill a fellow" or "Red on black, venom lack."

If a (suspected) poisonous snake bites someone, it's best to seek qualified medical help. Identify the snake if possible, but don't try to chase and kill it; don't risk another bite.

If it will be impossible to get to a doctor within 40 minutes, you may decide to use your emergency snakebite kit, but be aware that opinions vary on the effectiveness or safety of this treatment. Most recommended is the Sawyer Extractor Pump. If used within a few minutes of a bite, it can remove much of the injected venom.

The good news: Only a very small number of snakebites are fatal.

# FIRST AID

Buy, or put together, a first-aid kit. Include a book with up-to-date instructions for treating common outdoor problems.

*Blisters:* Wash with soap and water; cover with a Band-Aid or moleskin to protect. Don't prick the blister; the fluid will be absorbed as the blister heals, and you don't want to invite infection.

*Bruises:* Apply cold packs for 10- to 15-minute periods for a few hours, to reduce pain and swelling.

*Burns:* If hair or clothing is burning, use a towel or blanket to smother the fire; roll the victim on the ground if necessary. For first- or second-degree burns (red, possibly blistered skin; resembles a bad sunburn), run cold water over the area for 15 minutes, or immerse in a basin with cold water. Wash, rinse, and keep site elevated. Cover burn area if it needs protection from dirt or friction. Give aspirin for pain. See a doctor if bad blistering develops. For third-degree burns (deep, very serious): Do not hold under cold water. Cover with a clean dressing or sheet, and go to a doctor.

*(continued on page 80)*

rattlesnake

cottonmouth
(water moccasin)

# Health and Safety Tips

## Lost and Found

- It takes seconds for a small child to wander away. In a populated campground, all available campers generally form one big search party, to bring a quick and happy reunion.
- Sew or stamp identification on the inside of a child's clothes. A stick-on label (changeable) could show your site number, too, especially important whenever surnames are different.
- Children might like to wear a personalized bracelet, or "child tag" around the neck.

## Sun Protection

- Use sunscreen on cloudy days, too; 80 percent of UV rays may penetrate cloud cover.
- Use a lip balm with a strong sunscreen.
- Don't forget to apply sunscreen to ears.
- The hours between eleven and two o'clock (sun time, not daylight savings) are the worst for burning.
- Wet clothing doesn't provide the same sun protection as dry. You'll burn faster through the wet fabric. See the Clothing Tips sidebar on page 65, for clothing made especially for super-sun-sensitive skin.
- Sunglasses do more than prevent squint lines. The most obvious harm from ultraviolet rays is early cataracts. Look for lenses that screen out 99 percent of UV; 95 percent is not good enough.
- A wraparound frame style gives best protection, blocking sun from all angles.
- When you're hiking or boating, wear an eyeglass strap to keep glasses safe. Polarizing lenses will cut reflected glare.
- If you want to see the truest colors, choose gray lenses; green and brown are the next best. Blue and purple distort natural colors.
- Certain prescription drugs increase your sun sensitivity: tetracycline and some other antibiotics; diuretics; tranquilizers. Ask your pharmacist about any drugs you take regularly.

## Problem Plants, Bugs, and Snakes

- Touching the leaves of "poisonous" plants transfers the invisible irritant, urushiol oil, to your skin. If possible, wash it off right away, and you may prevent the rash. (Use Tecnu cleanser, rubbing alcohol, or mild soap and rinse with lots of water.)
- Learn to recognize the plants so you can avoid them. Poison ivy and poison oak both grow in three-leaf sections. Poison ivy berries are translucent white clusters.
- If you're walking through an area where these plants grow, stay covered up as best you can.
- If your clothes touch the plants, wipe them with alcohol, too.
- Use cool water, calamine lotion, alcohol, or witch hazel to relieve the itching.
- For sunburn, windburn, rashes caused by poisonous plants, or bug bites, try vinegar (four parts water to one part vinegar), tea (cooled, strong solution), baking soda (mixed with water and applied as paste), or aloe (gel from the plant, or any lotion).
- Most diseases associated with mosquitoes are problems in tropical climates. In North America, regional outbreaks of encephalitis ("sleeping sickness") have been blamed on mosquitoes. Recently, cases of the West Nile virus have been documented in some northeastern states. Most people experience only mild, flu-like symptoms, but it can result in fatal encephalitis. (See pages 46–47 and 74–75 on mosquito control.)
- Natrapel is a citronella-based insect repellent with aloe. Citronella is so safe, the FDA has approved it as a food additive.
- A relative newcomer to bug-chasing is called Bug Chaser. Its insect repellent is worn in a wristband—an appealing alternative. The main ingredient is Limonene—also FDA approved as a flavoring substance.
- Repellents with low DEET concentrations are marketed for children. Check with the pediatrician if you're concerned about its use.
- For protection when you need it (especially against ticks), DEET concentration should be at least 30 percent. Some brands go over 90 percent.
- While questionable as a fashion statement, the mosquito hood is a necessity in some places at some times, like rainy season in the Everglades. You can also buy an entire suit—jacket and pants—made of nylon mesh, to coordinate with the hat.
- Bad as they seem to people, mosquitoes are a first link in many a food chain: fish and fowl, reptile and mammal.

# Health and Safety Tips (continued)

- Try not to swat at bees; the movement might aggravate them.
- If you get into a swarm of bees, try to back away slowly; then lie face down on the ground and cover your face with your hands. Or, run for a bunch of bushes; the bees may not be able to separate your motion from that of moving branches.
- If you should have a mild allergic reaction to a bee sting (swollen finger or hand, itching palms or feet), take an over-the-counter antihistamine pill.
- Cover a bee sting with wet mud and let it dry on your skin. Some believe this draws out the poison. Others suggest it helps only because you can't scratch wet mud. Whichever, if it lessens the stinging temporarily, it's worth a little dirt.
- To help protect babies from biting bugs, keep nylon netting over the portable playpen.
- When walking through wooded or grassy areas, wear long-sleeved shirts, with rubber bands around wrists; long pants should be tucked into or taped to socks. Use tick repellent on your clothes, not on your skin. Don't forget repellent on shoes and socks. Walk in the middle of paths, and avoid overhanging branches and tall grass.
- After a hike through the bush, everyone participates in a tick check, in a true example of family togetherness. At first, you may feel vaguely uncomfortable about behavior usually associated with chimpanzees, but you get over it quickly, when you consider the consequences of ignoring this part of camping.

The larger ticks are obvious, but the deer ticks are not so easy to recognize. A magnifying glass helps you see the rounded shape with legs.

- You can buy special scissors/tweezers with beveled jaws that fit under and around the tick, to ease removal of the larger ticks.
- If tweezer tick-removal is not entirely successful, the tick's head stays under your skin. You may need to ask a doctor to remove it, to prevent or to treat infection.
- Wear ankle-high shoes or boots in poisonous-snake country. When not on a well-worn path, watch where you step. (You may want to use a stick to serve notice that a foot is soon to follow.)
- Canoeists should watch for water moccasins on overhanging limbs, tree roots, stumps, and logs.
- Bring—and study—a field guide for snake identification. Before you go into a particular wilderness habitat, you should know what snakes live there and how to recognize them.

## First Aid

Picnic foods or a different water source might bring on a stomach upset, but such minor upsets usually clear up in a day or two. Prolonged vomiting, however (longer than 24 hours), can lead to dehydration, a potentially life-threatening condition. Give plenty of water and fruit juices. Also see "Cooking Tips and Food Safety," page 160. Severe diarrhea will cause the same dehydration problem; if it lasts longer than two days, see a doctor.

Checklist for your first-aid kit:

- \_\_ Alcohol swabs
- \_\_ Disinfectant (alcohol or hydrogen peroxide)
- \_\_ First-aid cream
- \_\_ Aspirin or acetaminophen
- \_\_ Ibuprofen (anti-inflammatory)
- \_\_ Antihistamine
- \_\_ Antacid
- \_\_ Anti-diarrheal
- \_\_ Calamine lotion
- \_\_ Bug bite treatment
- \_\_ Bug repellent
- \_\_ Sunscreen
- \_\_ Sunburn treatment
- \_\_ Band-Aids
- \_\_ Moleskin
- \_\_ Gauze
- \_\_ Adhesive tape
- \_\_ Tweezers
- \_\_ Cotton swabs
- \_\_ Eye patch
- \_\_ Elastic bandage
- \_\_ Snakebite kit (if desired)
- \_\_ Oil of cloves (for toothache)
- \_\_ Personal medications

(continued from page 77)

*Cuts and Scrapes:* Minor bleeding usually stops in a few minutes. If not, press a gauze pad over the wound for about five minutes. Wash with soapy water, disinfect, and cover.

*Eye Injury:* If something is embedded in the eye, cover it with an inverted paper cup, to prevent further problems, and go to a doctor.

*Fish Hook:* If the barb is still visible, back it out. If the barb is too far into the skin, push it all the way through; cut the barb off, then pull the rest of the hook out. (Also, check date of last tetanus shot.)

*Nosebleed:* Sit down and lean head forward. Pinch the nose and hold 10 minutes; if it's still bleeding, try an ice pack over the nose for 10 minutes. Or, soak a cotton ball with water and place in nostril.

*Punctures:* Wash well and disinfect. These are very susceptible to infection. See a doctor; you may need a tetanus shot.

*Splinters:* If you can see the end, sterilize the tweezers and remove. If you can't see it, put some adhesive tape over the site, and pull.

*Sprains and Strains:* A joint may be sprained, a muscle strained; symptoms are the same: pain, swelling, bruising. Apply ice; support the area with an elastic bandage. In case of a suspected fracture, fabricate a splint with anything that will restrict movement of the affected area.

# ANIMAL CAMPERS

## 11

Cats don't seem to care about camping out, which is probably a good thing, considering what their claws could do to a nylon tent. They'll probably be happier staying home.

Many dogs, however, love to camp. Running through woods, splashing through water, chasing rabbits, ducks, or leaves—you can almost see them smile. And since part of their job is to make *us* smile, camping gives them plenty of chances to shine.

If your dog is a happy camper, take him along for everyone's fun, but only if you have checked in advance to be sure he will be welcome at your intended campground. Having a pet along does limit the places where you can stay. Some campgrounds will ask you to keep the dog leashed, but in some areas, pets aren't allowed at all, especially in government parks. A lapse of dog etiquette is part of the reason; camping neighbors don't want to listen to dogs barking or be confronted with dog mess. A more official explanation is that dogs might upset the wild creatures in the park, and from the perspective of a rabbit or duck, that's an understandable concern. To avoid disappointment, assign "dog check" to someone in the family. As long as you call ahead before each camping trip, you won't have to change destinations at 8:00 P.M.—when available campsites are few, and you'd really rather be settled into camp.

## BE PREPARED

If your pet is bothered by motion sickness, ask the veterinarian about possible preventives. Test the tranquilizing medications well ahead of an actual driving trip, to see how the dog responds. Find out how frequently the medication can be given.

When a vacation trip will take you far from home, you might want a printout of your pet's general health records, especially if there is a recurring problem. If the dog shows signs of illness while you're traveling, the new veterinarian will have a professional background report from which to start diagnosis. Naturally, you'll pack any pills or medication that your pet may need.

Interstate transportation of pets is regulated; you're required to have a health certificate stating that your pet has had shots updated annually, even if nobody ever asks to see it. File the health certificate in the glove compartment under Pet Passport. (You *will* need to show applicable health certificates to cross into Canada.)

## FEEDING STATION

Soon after setting up your tent, set up a feeding station for the dog. Carefully determine the best place for food and water dishes (convenience is less important than traffic flow). Think about giving the dog a plastic place mat; when he knocks food out of the dish, he won't get a muddy muzzle as he rummages around the ground chasing a kibble or bit of food.

## DOG WALK

Make up a discreet but complete dog walk kit to use while traveling and at the campground. (Many places will have dedicated pet-walk areas.) Include the deluxe Pooper Scooper, encased in its own plastic carry bag, plus a few empty plastic bags and some paper toweling, all contained in a handled bucket (a child's beach toy is a good size) or a small tote bag, also plastic lined. Keep the kit handy in the car or next to the tent.

## DOG RUN

When tying the dog outside, attach the leash to a line tied between two trees or poles. Arrange it so the dog can reach his water dish and a shaded place to sleep. To prevent a maypole wraparound, put a stop at each end of the run line, just short of each tree.

## DOG WASH

If the dog is allowed inside the tent, keep a doggy mat at one side of the entrance. Hang a doggy mop-up cloth nearby. After daily walks, dry the dog's feet, tummy hair, and ear-bottoms, if applicable, to keep excess dampness, dirt, and doggy smell out of the tent.

Even the outdoor dog may require a bit more care. After an afternoon of romping through wetland, the dog's coat will be a mess of leaves, mud, and twigs. Before the mess dries into a mass of tangles, brush out most of the foreign objects, or the dog will have some really bad hair days.

## Pet Precautions

- If your pup is one who does not react well to new situations, find a dog sitter and leave Rover in familiar territory. Nobody will have fun if you're all worried about the dog.
- On a hot summer day, you can't leave a dog in the car while you do some last-minute shopping. If it's 85°F outside, the temperature inside can reach over 100°F in 10 minutes, even if the windows are cracked open.
- Your dog's size will no doubt dictate how much dog gear you bring, but if he is accustomed to sleeping in a basket, try to pack it, or at least the cushion from inside the basket.
- You might as well bring some familiar amusements, too: a pull toy or a fetch toy, in case the dog doesn't like the choice of local sticks.
- Brush cornstarch, baking soda, or cedar sawdust through the dog's coat for a quick, dry shampoo.
- When dog fur mats around a burr, squeeze the burr with pli-

ers before trying to brush it out. Try softening the burr with vegetable oil. Vegetable oil dilutes dirty oil or tar spots, too; soak first, then wash with soap and rinse well.
- Keep the vacationing dog in a harness so there's no chance of slipping a collar.
- A carabiner (snap-hook) fastener on the end of the dog's leash makes it easy to quickly hook onto a door handle, a table leg, whatever.
- Attach a 35 mm film canister to the collar, and keep written information inside. You can easily change the date, location, campground name, and site number as you move.
- Like people, dogs shouldn't over-exert in hot, humid weather; dogs can suffer heat exhaustion, too. Keep the water dish filled.
- Dust the dog liberally with flea powder, as much for tick repelling as for flea control. A Lyme-preventing vaccine is available for dogs (see page 76).
- If your dog gets into a spat with

an animal—whether a pet or a raccoon—first try shouting or hand-clapping, then use water. Don't get too close to the combatants; a bucket or hose will deliver your message effectively.
- Pack a dog first-aid book. Your veterinarian's office may have free booklets, or call 800-252-7022 for a list of publications available from Heinz Pet Products.

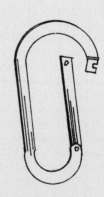

*Carabiner fastener in open position.*

*A small mat inside the tent will keep dirt—and the dog's sharp nails—off the tent floor.*

# LOST AND FOUND

A lost pet is every owner's worst nightmare, but one aspect seldom considered is how to prove that a found pet is really *your* pet. Without unremovable identification, you can't. Though the problem relates more to stolen pets than lost pets, the solution works for either. The pet gets a tattoo (number, not pictures) and is then registered with the National Dog Registry. When found animals are reported, owners and pets are reunited. The service is covered by a one-time fee: call 800-637-3647 for information. (The ID can also be done by microchip instead of tattoo.)

For a more traditional "lost" precaution, put finding information on an ID tag attached to the pet's collar, or written directly on a fabric collar or plastic flea collar. Consider the printed information carefully. When traveling, your car license number (and state) may be more useful than a home address. A phone number should belong to someone who's available to answer a call. A picture of the dog will help search efforts by camping neighbors.

# FOREST FRIENDS

People know about skunk evasion; some unfortunate dogs don't. If your dog chases the wrong black-and-white stripes, the aftermath quickly becomes your problem, too. Traditional stench removal attempts involve tomato juice (rub into dog's fur, then rinse and rinse and rinse) or diluted lemon juice or vinegar (mix 1 to 10 with water, and wash, always being careful of the dog's eyes).

Another woodland dweller might leave your dog with a face full of barbed porcupine quills. It's best to have a veterinarian remove the quills; the dog will be in pain and hard to handle. If you *must* try it yourself, use pliers to grasp each quill and work it back out with a steady, twisting pull. Cutting off the quill ends may help; they're hollow and, with ends cut, more flexible. Apply antiseptic to each puncture wound to ward off infection.

Try to avoid such a confrontation; don't let the dog wander around alone.

# PART THREE

# THE
# CAMPING

EUREKA

# PLAN AND PACK

## 12

You've practiced with the backyard tent-out. Maybe you traded yards with a neighbor, or joined up with cousins for a change of scenery. You gobbled marshmallows, gazed at stars, and even managed to get some sleep. Now, where should you go with your newfound experience?

## PLAN

While camping weekends shouldn't follow any rigid schedule, a certain amount of planning may be necessary. Where you camp may depend on whether you reserved a site; what you eat will depend on the food you brought.

Initially, new campers should base their choice of camping spots on "easy" factors: easy to find, easy to get to, easy to camp in. With those considerations as a starting point, "first" campgrounds are often those with all the home comforts and more: water, electricity, bathrooms, a self-service laundry, plus swimming pool or lake, maybe a fish pond, and a bunch of organized activities for kids and adults, including pony rides and hot-air balloon flights, if that's your pleasure. The campground amenities are there if you want them, but you can also stay in your corner of the woods and *camp*.

Later, as the details of camping become second nature, you'll look for different places: less-crowded campgrounds, more wild surroundings; canoe-in sites instead of drive-in.

### Activity Plan

Try to involve the whole family in the planning stages, so everyone will have a chance at his or her special interest. Individual parks often have a special focus—a site with historic or cultural significance, or a nature phenomenon like caverns or springs. Ecologic habitats are a fairly recent theme; any of these might fit into a child's next-year school project, or anybody's hobby interest.

Make a list of possible destinations. Call area chambers of commerce and ask for their travel package. If you're an AAA member, ask for suggestions and pick up some of their free maps and travel guides. Scan travel books and special-interest magazines at the library; write to park systems of all government levels. Later, word-of-mouth or networking with other campers will reveal lesser-known places. Area newspapers are often good sources of information for nearby places of interest. Ask at a local camping supply store; owners are usually experienced campers, and a good source of advice on destinations as well as equipment. Eventually, you'll have more ideas than you can possibly follow up, at least in one season.

Once you've chosen a campground, call to find out what you can see and do on your own, and what informational or organized tours might be available. If it's a government park, these can be anything from a wetland walk/plant study to a snake handling/feeding session guided by a ranger, naturalist, or interpreter.

It's been our experience that these walk-and-talks are not lecture-type monologues; the people are usually very involved with their subject, and enthusiastic about sharing their knowledge. Nature *is* a wonder and, properly presented, captures everyone's imagination.

## Money Plan

When calling parks, ask about all fees, so there will be no surprises. (Fees for entry, camping, and possibly other special uses are usually separate.) Find out if reservations are needed or even accepted, or if time is limited; some campgrounds (or individual sites) are first come, first camp.

## Circle Plan

A common mistake people make in vacation planning is not recognizing their own local attractions. People are often unfamiliar with the special features of their own hometown, county, state. In the great location exchange of summer, one group of travelers will go great distances to leave what other vacationers come similar distances to find.

Camping gives you a good way to stop your part of that cycle. Plan a summer of weekend visits to places within a 50- or 100-mile drive from home. Get a local map, one with lots of "gray" roads (the county routes, or back roads); draw a circle with your home as center, and the chosen mileage as radius. Study the outlined area to see what you can see, then plan a different location each weekend.

From a practical standpoint, you won't waste a lot of time driving, and you won't use a lot of gas. You may find water routes you didn't know

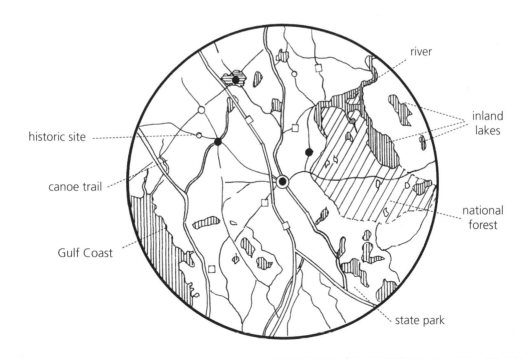

*Look for weekend campsites located within a 50- or 100-mile radius from home.*

existed. Every weekend may not be great, but you'll probably find some places you'll choose to bring visiting friends on their next vacation. Perhaps the best advantage is that you'll vacation all summer, not just for one two-week trip.

## Special Plan

Camping trips can also be planned around a special-interest event, like a horse show, an orchid exhibit, or a model plane fly-in. Dad, Mom, or whichever child has the special interest can attend the meeting/competition/festival while the rest of the family stays and plays at camp. Everybody wins.

## Food Plan

The family planning sessions should include some suggestion of individual responsibility regarding food shopping, cooking, and cleanup. Just don't use the word *responsibility*; *food* works much better. Ask everyone to volunteer preparing one meal. You may have to insist on veto rights, but you also may be surprised by a fun cookout combination. The shopping list thus becomes a family affair and less of a chore, and the older children can help with the actual shopping.

Some weekends, you may extend your family group when one of the children brings a friend. Be sure to include the friend in the food plan (parents,

# Friday Pack-and-Go Planner

It's Friday noon. The weather forecast shows nothing but sunshine and warmth, and by some miracle, the family's calendar is blank for the next two days. That's an opportunity that cannot be ignored—an impromptu camping trip might be just the thing to fill that void.

By 3, your thoughts are alternating between woodland hiking or lakeside loafing. You can almost hear the muffled sound of wind in the pines, almost feel the gentle breeze coming across the water. Three-ten is a good time for phone calls to see if the rest of the family is up for a weekend adventure. After all, spontaneous fun is often the best, right?

If this whim strikes you in mid-May or late September, you'll probably be able to just pack up and go. But reality intrudes if the idea strikes you in July or August. Pause long enough for a couple more phone calls to guarantee you will have a site to set on. Choose a place within a two-hour drive, so you'll not be too tired to set up camp or too crabby to enjoy it.

Four-thirty and you're home-

ward bound, making a mental list of who's going, what's going, and can they, you, and it all be out the door by 6? Sure, it can be done, but it probably depends on some prior preparation.

This is why you carefully store all the camping gear in one accessible place; this is why all the tent parts are close together and obviously visible, why all the sleeping bags are lined up and identified by owner, why all the food preparation things are organized by category. Just pick and pack.

A quick one- or two-day trip requires only minimal gear: tent, bed, clothes, lights. Don't bother with a lantern that requires fuel; take a lantern-battery lamp and use flashlights for backup. You need a way to keep food and a way to cook it. A toothbrush is important; a shower kit and towel are nice, though not essential.

You need the tent, but you don't need any add-on vestibules or annexes or tarps. A sleep mat and sleeping bag for each camper are necessities, but everyone can use a corner of a duffel bag or a rolled-up

sweatshirt for a pillow. Use your smallest duffel—it will help to keep you from bringing along stuff you don't need. One change of clothes should do; Friday outfits can be repeated on Sunday. Of course, iffy weather might suggest bringing a long and a short version of your one change of clothes, and the usual sweater and jacket combination allows for whatever number of layers might be required.

Plan meals that can be cooked on a grill, whether it's the campground's or your own smallest portable. That eliminates most pots and pans. Take one big frying pan and possibly one small saucepan to heat water for coffee or the few dishes you may use. Plan finger food meals to eliminate the need for most dishes: omelet-bagels for breakfast; assorted sandwiches or snacks for lunch; burgers, chicken, or kabobs for supper, with side dishes of veggies also kabobbed or wrapped in foil packets to steam at the edge of the grill. (If someone insists on a side dish that can't be foil-cooked, use the time-honored open-can-on-the-grill method.)

too, if necessary). You don't need surprises like food allergies, restricted diet, or just plain likes and dislikes when you're a long way from a grocery store.

## Over-Plan

Don't over-plan a vacation camping trip. The idea is to relax and enjoy, not set speed records for tent setup and take-down.

Young children still need regularly timed rest, whether they admit it or not. When they're tired, they're unhappy, and too soon, everyone else will follow their grouchy lead.

## Base Camp Plan

Some families spend their annual vacation at a base camp, taking daytime driving trips from "home" to see the area sights. A better escape from all the stresses of ordinary life is to stay at camp; the only moving around is done on foot, or possibly on water.

## PACK

Whether camping for the weekend or a month, you still need the same basic equipment. While the mounds of gear stacking up in the driveway look intimidating, think about jigsaw puzzles, and start fitting.

# Friday Pack-and-Go Planner (continued)

In the camping storage corner, keep a small box or bag with basics for these occasions: paper plates, cups, and paper towels (napkins). A second bag or box should have charcoal (self-starting), foil, and matches. A third holds silverware, utensils, and any cups or bowls that might be deemed essential by particular family members.

Another option regarding most of the food preparation items is to simply buy them when you buy the food, which cuts down the number of things to pack from home. If you buy individual-sized containers of all drinks (juice, tea, milk, soda) you can ignore the paper cups completely.

The cooler should be the last thing to go into the car, so it is accessible when you want to fill it at the grocery store. Truly organized people may already have a master grocery list for such occasions. If you are not among them (and assuming there's an adequately stocked grocery store on the road to the campground), make up the shopping list in the car as you travel. If the grocery store is next door to a gas station, one stop can take care of all fill-ups. It will probably be too late for a camping supper, but a deli roast chicken with side salads can make a picnic on the way. On a summer day, you'll be at camp before dark, allowing time to set up and settle in.

If you always keep a first-aid kit in your car, you won't have to remember to pack one. Two more "always-carries" could be sunscreen and insect repellent. A flashlight is usually a permanent car fixture already; binoculars could be too.

## CHECKLIST

___ Tent
___ Poles
___ Stakes
___ Sleeping bags
___ Mats
___ Smallest duffel packed with fewest clothes possible
___ Shower kit
___ Towel
___ Toilet tissue
___ Battery lantern
___ Flashlight(s)
___ Grill

___ Charcoal
___ Aluminum foil
___ Matches

*"Paper and plastic" box*
___ Paper plates
___ Paper cups
___ Paper towels
___ Resealable plastic storage bags
___ A few tall kitchen trash bags
___ Water bottle

*Cooking things*
___ Silverware
___ Utensils
___ Knife
___ Can opener
___ Skewers
___ Tongs
___ Spatula
___ Cups/bowls
___ Cooler
___ ICE!

*Car things*
___ First-aid kit
___ Sunscreen
___ Insect repellent
___ Flashlight
___ Binoculars

## Inside Organizers

Whether in the car or at the campsite, stackable boxes keep similar items organized—cooking equipment, canned goods, lanterns. Sleeping bags and duffels either stack or stuff.

Though you risk earning the dubious title of "bag-person," a few canvas tote bags are practical for toting stuff that doesn't lend itself to organized stacking. Fresh food items are easier to carry, too.

When you're ready to pack, gather all gear in the driveway. This is your best chance for eliminating items on the no-argument basis of no room. (If you'll be transferring gear to a canoe, try to pack according to *its* carrying capacity.) When all nonessentials have returned to their respective closets, consider how you'll set up camp, and pack accordingly: last in, first out. The duffels and sleeping bags stay cleaner sitting in the car than on the ground; plus, the less you must handle your gear, the more energy you'll have to set up camp.

## Outside Carriers

A cartop carrier can accommodate a lot of extra gear, but don't be surprised if it affects your gas mileage. Some designs are more aerodynamic, to minimize wind resistance. Carriers clamp onto brackets, but most campers add tie-downs for security.

One family built a custom storage bin (8 x 4 x 2 feet high) to fit atop their aging station wagon. The box was carefully fiberglassed, so no water could sneak inside. Though hardly an engineering marvel, it could hold a windsurfer.

A luggage rack gives you a platform and tie bars to hold whatever you want to load on top. A waterproof tarp, securely tied, is a necessity. Use a lot of stretchy tie-downs, or the flapping will drive you bonkers.

Ski racks can work for "baggage" other than skis.

To carry a boat or a canoe cartop, the most basic tie-down uses four foam pads for cushioning and ropes tied in inverted Vs in front and back, connecting boat to car bumper.

For a custom-fitted rack, check Yakima (800-472-3353). This manufacturer has a full line of components to customize a rack system for your model vehicle. They make bicycle racks, too; if the cartop's occupied, consider front or back racks for bicycles. Many tenting locations are ideal places for country biking.

With any cartop add-on, don't be surprised if you hear some unusual humming sounds when the car is moving. It's wind in the rigging.

# DRIVE

The gear's all packed, and the campers are seated in the best compromise arrangement; you hope the

*Gather all camping gear in one place. Those items needed first at camp should be packed last.*

# Car Travel Tips

### What to Bring

Pack car travel items in a separate tote bag so they don't get lost in the trunk. Picnic things, snacks, tissues should be handy.

Keep one small bag handy, with a change of clothes for everyone. If you arrive on a rainy night, you may look for a motel rather than settle for a wet-night tent setup, and you won't want to dig for and through individual duffels.

Each child can pack one small bag with toys, coloring books, reading books, writing paper, and pencils, for car time or rainy-day camp time. (If the bag is see-through, it's easier to locate.)

Bring along a stash of small garbage bags for travel trash, and dispose of it often.

In-car snacks don't have to be chips and pretzels; more salt means more drinks means more stops. Take cut fresh veggies, fruit (fresh or dried), nuts, peanut-butter crackers, your camp trail mix.

The map assortment will stow better if confined in one envelope or large zip-top bag. (Keep a smaller bag for the collection of travel and informational brochures you pick up along the way.)

Keep the cooler in the car rather than in the trunk and cover it with a blanket and a light-colored cloth to reflect heat. It will stay cooler longer. It also helps to buy specially made heat/sun reflectors for your rear windows.

If your car is not equipped with a separated coin holder, use 35 mm film canisters. Quarters fit perfectly, but at least the dimes and nickels can be segregated, for easier counting at toll booths.

Especially when back-roading, have a spare-parts kit for the car: belts, fuses, hoses, tire quick-fix, tools, flares, jumper cables, duct tape. Some silver reflective tape comes in handy if a headlight goes: a strip of tape will show oncoming cars you're not a motorcycle.

Mount a small compass on the car dash. It helps you find a return road when you're turned around on some scenic back route.

Most campers bring more than they need. Each trip, decide what can be eliminated next time.

### What to Do

Counting spotted cows or purple cars is no challenge for today's computer kids, but tracking home states of other cars often gives them some information about the state: motto, state bird. And vanity plates can keep everyone amused for a time.

Driving time passes more quickly with a tape of favorite songs or books to play on the way (on car stereo or separate headsets, depending on the songs or books).

Make up a story about the place you're going. You may be surprised to hear the children's vision or expectation.

If an unsuspecting bee, hornet, or wasp gets blown into the car, practice "calm" so the children can learn by watching. Calmly watch the bug as the driver calmly slows the car to a stop, and calmly open all doors so passengers can calmly make their escape. Hopefully, someone will be brave and evict the unwitting intruder while it's still dazed.

---

lists were complete and the check marks right. Grab the dog, and go.

## Directions

The large-format road atlas (Rand McNally is a personal favorite) is usually all the map you *need*, but smaller-scale state or regional maps show you a lot more, particularly the back roads or scenic routes you may choose to follow. Many of these maps also have notes or symbols pointing out any special sights. (If your state tourism packet did not include maps, stop at the first large truck stop or a local bookstore.)

Even the larger-scale atlases show at least minimal camping information, usually in the form of a small triangle or teepee alongside a road. If your original travel plan is disrupted, you can find an alternate stopover. Most towns that have a vacation attraction have campgrounds as well as a motel row; though they may be more RV park than tent haven, you can at least find a spot for overnight.

Children like having their own road map. Even if they're not old enough to handle directing, they can watch and follow the turns you take, and learn exactly how to get lost.

As the older children show the inclination and

# Parks And Campgrounds

You could spend years marveling at nature's diversity in U.S. national and state parks, and Canadian national and provincial parks. Pick a surrounding: mountain or caverns; wetland or woodland; frozen tundra or barrier beach.

National parks typically charge an entry fee ($1 to $4 per person, or $3 to $10 per car) plus a user fee for a campsite. If you're over 62, you can apply for a Golden Age Passport, which allows free entry for everyone in your car to all federally operated recreation areas. (Those under 62 can purchase a Golden Eagle Passport. A $25 annual fee allows unlimited entry into any park, all year.) These are available from the National Park Service, the U.S. Forest Service, or the U.S. Fish and Wildlife Service. Purchasing the annual Federal Duck Stamp ($15) will get you into any national wildlife refuge. (Ask at the post office.) Even where wilderness campsites are free, you may need a permit. Always ask. See page 151 for addresses of managers of government lands.

Directories list thousands of private campgrounds, organized by state. Other guides list free camping places. Find the books at camping stores or in catalogs, or see page 148 for mailing addresses.

## When and Where to Go

Think about camping off season. It may be cheaper (at private campgrounds), and it will be less crowded. Autumn usually brings spectacular camping weather. You may have to carry gear some distance into wilderness campsites, but that slight disadvantage might mean the places will be less crowded.

At many campgrounds, you can rent a site for an entire season. Establishing such a "base camp" is a good introduction to the camping life. Set up your summer home early in your outdoor season, and go to it every weekend; from there, you can take day trips to sightsee (bring your bicycles), or stay at camp and—*camp*. As long as you're all at camp, the family will spend regular, quality time together.

Pick a location close enough for easy weekending. Choose a good-sized, divided-room wall tent, or be creative: find a facsimile of the pyramid teepee shape or the igloo-like Mongolian yurt (call or write Pacific Yurts, 77456 Highway 99 South, Cottage Grove, OR 97424; 800-944-0240; www.pacificyurts.com).

Planning a weekend's activity is good up to a point. Leave some open time for individual moods or surprise discoveries.

ability, let them help with navigation. The worst that can happen is you'll be temporarily misplaced, not an unusual event, and they may spot a side-road site you've missed.

## Slow Road

On vacation weeks, too many families run marathon 500-mile days, just to be done with the driving. For most, the next day is wasted because everybody's tired, stiff, and cranky. Better to choose a closer destination if time is too limited to allow relaxed traveling.

Make the effort to drive back roads, and you'll feel like you've gone through a time warp or twi-light zone. There are still places where you can drive for hours and not see the lineup of familiar logos—no fast-food drive-ins, no discount stores or motel chains. You'll see roadsides instead of road signs, scenery instead of cement. Hometown USA is alive and well just a few miles from the interstate.

## Diversions

Try to buy your fresh fruit and vegetables at a farm stand along the way to camp. Not only will the local produce taste better, it will probably be a relative bargain, too. (Plus, you're symbolically moving away from the city and supermarket express lanes.)

*Travel scenic byways instead of expressways.*

If you're driving during daytime hours, break the fast-food habit and have a picnic lunch. (If quitting cold-turkey is too much for your family, compromise with an ice cream stop for dessert.)

Try to plan your arrival at camp before dark. Of course, you practiced putting up the tent in the dark, but it's so much easier by daylight rather than by flashlight.

# COOKOUT FIRES

## 13

Outdoor cooking is not difficult, nor is it necessarily different from ordinary food preparation. If you choose to use a two-burner camp stove, cooking outside is just like cooking inside, except you're working on a smaller surface with fewer pots. At home, how often do you really need four burners to cook a meal? Even then, it's by preference, not necessity, with the possible exception of those occasions when you're fixing sit-down dinners for 16.

If you choose to cook over a campfire, you can easily adapt your home cooking methods to the different heat source. Cooking times may vary, and you may use different cooking pots, but basic recipes remain the same.

However you prepare the food, be assured everyone will enjoy it. Eating becomes one of the more memorable parts of camping. Whether increased exercise whets the appetite, or cooking aromas are more enticing in the open air, interest in mealtime is definitely more noticeable. If at home you eat because it's habit, at camp you'll eat because you're hungry. Cookout conversations are often dotted with remember-when details of roasting the duck or steaming the fish over campfire coals. Best of all, cooking may cease to be a chore, as it becomes a can-you-top-this challenge. Men who happily ignore the home kitchen suddenly take pride in becoming preparer as well as provider, often experimenting with flavor combinations that regular cooks would never consider. Children who can't manage to find hot dogs in the refrigerator suddenly find the ability to put together real meals, with only a little help from a mom.

## COOKSTOVES

Most camping families will use a two-burner camp stove. When folded for transport, the stove is about the size of an attaché case, and is similarly equipped with a convenient carrying handle. When set up to use, the lid stands at a 90-degree angle to

COLEMAN COMPANY, INC.

*Compact two-burner stoves take the hassle out of camp cooking. Available in liquid-fuel or propane models.*

# Camp Stoves

- Folding stands are made to hold camp stoves. While not a necessity, you might like the convenience of cooking at a familiar standing level. (Some stands have a pot-or-food-holding shelf about midway between base and stove platform.)
- When the stove is closed for carrying, pack an oven mitt (or a dish towel) between the burners and the pot platform, to stop a lot of metal rattling.
- Some propane stoves have "electronic ignition," described as a high-tech version of rubbing two rocks together to create a spark, the rocks being a crystal and a hammer.
- If there's no built-in sparkmaker, you'll use long matches or a gas lighter (sparks like a cigarette lighter, looks like a letter opener).
- Propane is also known as LPG or liquefied petroleum gas.
- When pouring liquid fuels, use a funnel for less chance of spillage.

- Coleman sells a filter/funnel, to help keep impurities out of the stove.
- Don't store liquid fuel for any length of time (not in the can and especially not in the stove), or it may get gummy. If you use the stove every week or two, there's no problem, but burn out all fuel before seasonal storage.
- Liquid-fuel stoves sometimes need help. Carry spare parts and whatever tools you'd need to put in the parts. (Kit could include gasket and/or O-ring, spare jet, cleaning pad, and jet-cleaning needle.) The pressure-pump plunger should be lubricated regularly with a light-grade machine oil.
- Reread stove instructions and maintenance tips before each trip, and bring trouble-shooting instructions with you.
- The backpacker's standard, a one-burner stove can be carried in a daypack on a hike, so you

can have soup or hot chocolate on a cool day.
- If you want a one-burner stove as a backup, you have plenty to choose from: besides stoves that use propane/butane or stove fuel/unleaded gas, there are those that burn kerosene or alcohol. (Alcohol stoves are the safest type, but they're not noted for high heat.)
- Classic emergency camp cooking is done on a small fold-up metal platform that sits over a can of Sterno ("canned" heat, alcohol based, occasional use only).
- The Sierra stove from ZZ Corp. will burn charcoal, wood, or other solid fuels.
- If your emergency stove is a one-burner, use it anytime you want a third burner—rather then buy the bulk of a three-burner stove.
- The versatile Pyromid burns any solid fuel (charcoal, wood, Sterno) or butane. Use its one burner as a grill, stove, oven, or smoker.

the cooking surface, to provide a back-wall wind block. Side panels can be popped into position if a breeze continues to threaten the flame. Camp stoves sit conveniently on a picnic table, a level rock, or on the ground (under the tent's awning when it's raining).

Regardless of their fuel source, all two-burner camp stoves have a similar compact shape. Those that burn liquid fuel (kerosene, unleaded gas, or Coleman fuel, aka white gas) have an attached cylindrical fuel tank. Those that burn propane use disposable propane bottles, or are connected to a larger, refillable propane tank.

## Propane

Propane stoves are the easiest camp stoves to use because they are the most familiar, especially if you use a gas stove or grill at home. While you may need to use a match or other spark to light the burner (pilot lights not being portable), from then on it is cooking as usual: the knob adjusts for high or low heat, and cooking times will be fairly close to what you expect on a home stove. (Some models do have a built-in sparkmaker, eliminating the step of lighting the burner.)

Propane stoves are clean and efficient. A few campers shy away from carrying pressurized fuel, but the only other disadvantage is cost: propane, especially in the disposable bottles, is more expensive than other camp stove fuels. Many campers choose to use it, anyway; since outdoor cooking is a weekend thing, convenience takes precedence over frugality.

## Liquid Fuel

For the new camper, the less familiar cookstoves are those that burn liquid fuels. Some use only white gas; some dual-fuel models accept either white gas or plain, readily available automobile unleaded gas. These stoves are just as easy to cook over once they're burning, but they are not quite as easy to start as the propane stoves. While propane is already pressurized in the cylinder, with liquid-fuel stoves you must pressurize the fuel. This is accomplished with a simple pumping mechanism built into the tank. If you've followed the manufacturer's instructions carefully, you simply pump up pressure, turn the knob, and light the burner with a match.

A common problem with lighting these stoves stems from simple overfilling. Directions specify not to fill tanks completely. When you pump to pressurize, the idea is to mix air and fuel in order to vaporize the fuel. If the tank's too full, you'll get straight fuel at the burner, and the stove won't work.

Once you become comfortable with using a liquid-fuel stove, you'll find they provide the best heat; also, with unleaded gas as the fuel, they are the most economical to use.

## Choosing and Using

The fuels are commonly available. You can find unleaded gas anywhere, anytime; with propane and white gas, you'll need to time your purchase with the hours a store or gas company is open. Naturally, because they are so flammable, you must be especially careful with liquid fuels and their con-

tainers. Don't refill the stove tank if it's hot, and don't refill it anywhere near a possible source of a spark. Don't let the fuel tank itself get too hot; if you're using a separate wind screen, don't set it up so it reflects heat onto the fuel tank. Always light stoves at arm's length, in case of a flare-up.

Don't use stoves inside the tent or in any unventilated place. All fire uses oxygen, and produces odorless and deadly carbon monoxide.

When choosing a camp stove and cooking pots, visualize (and/or measure) the size pots the burners can hold at the same time. For example, on the two-burner stove, you can't use two big frying pans together, or a big frying pan and a spaghetti pot. The ordinary two-burner stove will hold one large and one small pot. Three-burner models are available, but before buying the extra size, be sure it will give you the extra cooking surface you're after.

Don't rely on advertised numbers to determine how much fuel you should take. On your first trips, take a lot; then keep track of what *you* use in a typical weekend.

Even better, use the stove to fix a few meals at home before taking it camping. You'll be familiar with lighting it and cooking on it. You'll know which pots fit; and if the pots overheat, you'll know to take a *flame tamer* (a slotted metal ring that diffuses flame) for simmering.

# WOOD FIRES

Fire-building techniques have already been covered in an earlier chapter (see pages 35–38). Once you have the desired hot coals, you can use the fire to cook *directly* (as in hot dogs on sticks, kabobs on skewers, or steaks on a grill) or *indirectly* (as the heat source for stewing, frying, baking, or steaming).

Even for this kind of camp cooking, you can use an assortment of pans from the home kitchen, the exception being the hang-over-the-fire meals. These require a sturdy top handle which ordinary pots from home do not have. Look for cooking kettles with lids as well as handles in camping stores.

## Tripod

The classic camp bean pot hangs from a *tripod* construction. Buy or make a tripod: Use three lengths

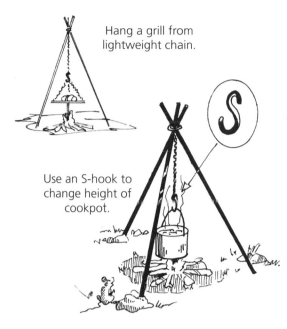

Hang a grill from lightweight chain.

Use an S-hook to change height of cookpot.

*Use a tripod support to hang a cookpot over the fire.*

of ½-inch or ¾-inch-diameter electrical conduit for the legs, each about 4 feet long. Clamp them together at the top; an electrical-fitting J-clamp works well. Use an appropriate length of lightweight chain to hang the bean pot, with an S-hook at each end. You can also add a grill to the tripod— square or round, whichever you find first. Attach pieces of chain to the corners of the grill, if square; or to the north, east, south, and west marks on a round grill. Connect the chain ends with one S-hook, and use another piece of chain and a second S-hook to hang the grill.

## Cooking Platform

Campfire cooking has many other forms. Simplest is the grill platform. Again, buy one or make one, recycling a grill from a burned-out barbecuer. Bend some V-shaped metal legs to hold it up, or prop it up on rocks. Then cook directly, by broiling (grilling); or indirectly, with frying pans, pots, or by heating the food right in the can (see page 105). Adjustable legs, rather than rigid ones, are very handy for uneven or rocky ground.

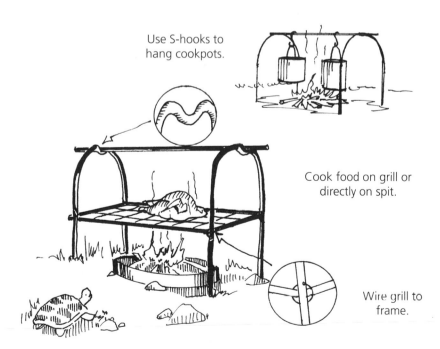

Use S-hooks to hang cookpots.

Cook food on grill or directly on spit.

Wire grill to frame.

*Cooking platform.*

97

*What could be more of a camping tradition than hot dogs cooked over the fire?*

Or, make a combination grill and spit. Use whatever metal tubing you may have (the electrical conduit bends easily) to form arched end stands. Attach the grill with rings at each corner; bend notches into the top of each end stand's arch so the spit rod stays in place. The spit must be sufficiently strong to hold the duck or beef roast you plan to cook on it. Also try Cornish hens: they cook much faster, a fact you'll appreciate when tantalizing aromas start wafting around the campsite.

The same outer structure could be used without the grill, in place of a tripod, if you should want to hang more than a single pot.

## Grill Helpers

In cooking directly on a grill, some foods may try to escape into the fire. Fish, burgers, shrimp, and other small items can easily fall through the wide voids in a grill top. Use a hinged, wire broiler basket to hold things inside; or add to the cooking surface with heavy-duty aluminum foil or foil baking tins, with a few holes punched through the bottom.

## Traditional Cook Fire

Fire-building know-how is covered in chapter 4, "Heat and Light." Start with a star or teepee type to build a keyhole fire, which supplies the cook with a ready and controllable source of heat. Keep the main fire in the rounded top section of the keyhole shape; push hot coals into the narrower bottom section, keeping them confined by rows of rocks or a couple of green logs. Place the logs in an open V shape (wide at fire end, narrower at coal end) so pots balance on them over the coals. Don't use shale or other porous riverbed rocks to line a fire; steam could cause an abrupt split, sending rock shards flying.

Build the fire only as large as you need to keep the coal supply adequate. Ventilation is the key to continued, controlled burning; stir the fire to let in more air, or close in the sides to keep flames down. (Too much ventilation, however, can be a problem. You can shelter your cook fire with a wind screen.) Cooking times will vary, depending partly on the wood you're burning; hardwoods provide longer-lasting coals. A deeper layer of coals would hasten cooking time, since more heat is more concentrated. You can also increase heat by knocking ashes off the coals, or just lower the cooking platform so the food is closer to the heat.

# CHARCOAL FIRES

In some locations, an open wood fire is not allowed, but charcoal smoldering in a fire pit is okay. This needn't change your cooking plans; the same methods and helps can be used over charcoal, too, and if you miss the woodsy smell or taste, toss in a few hickory chips, packed just for such occasions.

If the campground doesn't have individual fire pits, make your own from an old barbecue grill, the metal lid from a garbage can, or a cut-down 5-gallon can—whatever works. Line the charcoal holder with a shallow layer of gravel and cover it with a circle of aluminum foil. The gravel protects the base from constant burning; the foil catches food drippings and reflects heat back up to food. Unscented kitty litter can be used instead of gravel, and in the case of an already-burned-out grill bottom, you may need to line it with a double thickness of foil before adding the litter.

*In addition to its intended use, a grill can provide the heat source for cooking with a frying pan.*

## Charcoal Starters

Charcoal lighter fuel works, but it's been criticized as unhealthy for people and the environment. Alternative fire starters exist; they just require a little more effort than standing in the checkout lane. Considering that such alternatives are less of a fire hazard, help protect the environment, and are probably cheaper, the time and effort are well spent. (Self-starting charcoal is just presoaked with starter fluid, so it doesn't count as a reasonable alternative.)

You can make your own charcoal starters beforehand, using empty cardboard egg cartons. Cut apart top and bottom, and "glue" the egg-holding section into the inverted lid with a bit of melted paraffin. Then pour about ¼ inch of paraffin into each egg section. When you're ready to cook, set a charcoal briquette into each cup, pile more on top, and light the carton.

Another starter method uses a chimney made from a large can. Using tinsnips, cut away the bot-tom as well as the lid, and scallop the bottom edge to allow air to flow through. Crumple up some sheets of newspaper and put them into the bottom of the chimney. Put briquettes on top; light the newspaper, and it lights the charcoal. Later, remove the chimney with tongs or pliers, and spread out the coals.

Or, instead of scalloping the bottom edge of the can, cut six perpendicular slits up from the bottom, evenly spaced around the can. Bend up three of the sections (alternate bands), leaving three sections as "legs." The bent bands shape a small platform inside the can; the newspaper goes under, the charcoal on top of the platform. Air circulates freely; when the charcoal lights, lift off the can and spread the coals.

## Wind Shield

Whether you're cooking over a wood fire or a charcoal pit, a good wind can effectively defeat your purpose. You can buy a ready-made, three panel folding aluminum wind shield. Or, you can make a wind screen by fastening a piece of thin aluminum sheeting between two dowels (see below). Place the screen wherever it's needed, planting the dowel ends so the curve of aluminum blocks the wind.

Or, set up a shield of flat rocks.

## Pit Cooking

A Dutch oven gives you another way to cook with glowing coals— a modified form of pit cooking to

*Thin aluminum sheeting wired to conduit or dowels creates a wind screen.*

**99**

# Camp Cookery

- When you start camping, take your heaviest-weight pans from home. Cast iron is a favorite; heavy cast aluminum is okay, too. Later, you may buy a set just for camping (see next chapter).
- Bake quick breads, small cakes, muffins, and biscuits in a heavy (thick)-bottomed, covered frying pan. Grease the pan and dust with flour to help prevent burning. Use a flame tamer if necessary (a flat circle of metal, slotted to diffuse flame).
- Since your home kitchen won't likely have a set of saucepans with "bucket"-type bail handles, this is one item you'll need to buy if you intend to cook by the hanging-pot method. Look in camping supply stores and catalogs.
- Before setting pots on a grill or over an open fire, coat the underside with liquid dishwashing detergent; they'll be easier to clean later.
- Bring a separate storage bag/ stuff sack for fire-blackened cookware.
- Use a small-diameter metal pipe for a spit. Drill a few holes near the center so you can wire the food to the pipe; this way it will turn the food rather than spin around inside. Weld a handle onto the spit, for easier turning. For individual spit-cooking with skewers, get the twisted or angular metal, so food turns with the skewer and doesn't slip.
- No fireplace grill? Use a couple of flat metal bars, with the ends resting on the fire pit's outer circle of rocks. Space the bars close enough together so pots will rest securely on both without tipping.
- Keep water handy to retard cooking or to put out small flare-ups. A water pistol does a good job (if kept confined to business), or use a large baster, a pump spray bottle, or a salad dressing bottle with shaker top.
- A star fire—where you push burning logs into the center— allows you to control the heat. A teepee fire has a higher flame, good for cooking with a hanging pot. The log cabin fire burns fast, with more flame; better for heating or signaling than cooking.
- When using charcoal, a good rule of thumb is to use enough briquettes to cover a single layer slightly larger than the grill space filled by the food. Let the charcoal burn at least half an hour before cooking.
- When cooking something that requires long-term heat, keep a circle of briquettes around the perimeter of the initial fire, ready to push to the center as needed to maintain consistent heat. If the food cooks before the charcoal's burned, try saving the unspent fuel. Put it in a covered container to cut oxygen; or submerge it in water, then dry it out for reuse.
- An unusual type of charcoal grill looks like a steel bucket and cooks with newspaper—and the cooking fat drippings—as its fuel. It collapses and nests in three parts for smaller packing.
- Self-starting charcoal has been presoaked with starter fuel. If you're trying not to use starter fuel, this is not your answer. If you choose to use starter fuel anyway, don't add extra to a slow-starting fire. It won't help, and it could hurt. Don't ever substitute kerosene, gasoline, or any other solvent for starter fuel.
- Real pit cooking—like Dutch-oven roasting, but without a pot—was once popular with outdoor chefs (remember pig roasts?). But, with the emphasis on reducing impact on land, conscientious campers choose other cooking methods—with the possible exception of clambakes at low tide.
- Dutch ovens are made of cast iron or aluminum. The aluminum pots have the advantage of less weight and no rust. Cast iron converts insist aluminum does not cook as well. Dutch ovens are made in indoor and outdoor versions. The outdoor type has the legs and inverted lid for charcoal. Only Dutch ovens have the extra-thick sides that retain heat a long time. (You would not want to bury regular pots in charcoal; the handles—and possibly the food—would burn.) A Dutch oven can hang over an open campfire to be a giant bean pot or chili cooker.
- Use a shiny cookie sheet (or two) as reflectors to direct heat to a baking pan. On a chilly day, a reflector can also be used to direct heat into a tent doorway.
- Make a frame for some stainless steel wire mesh, and use it to keep delicate foods (like fish) from falling through the gaps in the grill.
- A grill-and-stove combination makes a versatile cooker. When open, one side is a grill, the

## Camp Cookery (continued)

other the stove; you can use both at the same time. While it doesn't fold up as compactly as an ordinary camp stove, you're ready for whatever type of cooking you want to do. Check Camping World catalog, 800-626-5944.

- Save the foil pans from cakes or frozen dinners to use at camp, for baking, steaming, reheating.
- Use foil to wrap rolls (or bread), and heat them at the side of the fire or grill. A double thickness of heavyweight aluminum foil can be used instead of a frying pan, especially when you don't want to wash the pan after frying bacon. Be careful not to poke holes through your "pan."

### Safety

- Always keep a bucket filled with water close to the fire to halt any major flare-ups.
- Always wear oven mitts or heavy-duty gloves when moving pans on and off the fire or grill. Some pot-lifter grips (available from camping suppliers) or lightweight pliers are a big help in moving pots.

- Don't try to burn Styrofoam meat trays, especially if you're using the fire for cooking; the melting foam sends off bad fumes. Similarly, plastic bags don't belong in fires.
- Never leave the fire smoldering if everyone leaves camp, no matter how short the time you expect to be gone. Douse the fire thoroughly, stir the ashes, and douse again. Repeat until you can touch the ground and feel no heat.

do in an existing fire pit. A large, heavy-duty cookpot, the traditional outdoor Dutch oven has legs to stand on and an edged lid that holds charcoal. To use, stand the pot portion in a bed of hot coals; put the food inside, the lid on top, and more hot coals on top of the lid. Now there is heat from above and below, creating a fairly uniform interior temperature in the pot/oven. Use a Dutch oven to roast meat, make stews, or bake whatever.

Dutch ovens work really well, but it may be too hot underneath if you don't scrape out some coals. Sometimes the fire-heated ground is enough. Also, a small shovel or trowel is handy for moving hot coals without scorching knuckles.

## BARBECUE GRILLS

Yet another cooking option is the familiar patio barbecue grill, charcoal or gas. You may already own a small portable table-top grill or hibachi; take it along for your outdoor cooking until you decide what kind of camp stove you want. Use it for grilling and also to heat standard camp fare like beans, soups, stews. If you don't already own a grill, it's a small investment that will see double use as the backyard backup.

If you'll be buying a small propane grill, get one that can be connected to a refillable propane tank; you'll get more cooking time for your dollars.

When you want to add a smoky flavor to your meal, the covered grill is the best way to do it. Use any flavor-enhancing wood. Soak a handful of chips in water for a few hours; put them on top of charcoal (after it has burned down) or wrap them

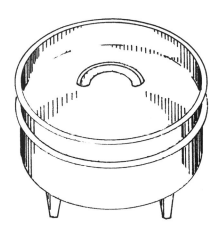

*A traditional Dutch oven has a recessed lid to hold hot coals. Coals also fit underneath; legs hold oven level.*

in foil, puncture the top of the foil packet, and place it on the grill. Close the cover for strongest flavor.

# STEAM HEAT

One more way to cook outside: forget the pots altogether. Think aluminum foil; wrap and steam food over any heat source.

Besides being easy to cook, steamed foods are healthy for you. Not to suggest they will be taste-less: country-style ribs foil-wrapped with your own barbecue sauce will have flavor steamed through the meat, not just sitting on top in a surface glaze. Using the heavyweight foil, wrap each packet securely, rolling up and folding in the side edges to seal in juices. Steam vegetables for dinner and fruit for dessert. Double-wrap any items that tend to burn easily. Wrap food with the shiny side of foil facing in, so heat won't be deflected back to the fire.

Cooking corn-on-the-cob in its own husk is fairly common around campfires, but other foods benefit from a natural wrap, too. Wrap meats or sliced vegetables in grape or cabbage leaves and steam/broil a subtle flavor into the food as it cooks.

# OUTDOOR OVENS

Outdoor baking can be done in a reflector oven, an arrangement whereby something shiny bounces heat onto a baking area.

A "permanent" reflector oven can be made with thin aluminum sheeting bent into a sideways V behind the baking shelf. Set up next to the fire, the shiny aluminum reflects heat up and down onto the top and bottom of the shelf where the item to be baked is placed.

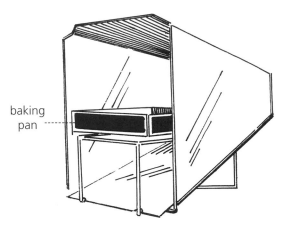

baking pan

*Place reflector oven in front of fire so all interior surfaces trap and reflect heat.*

For a temporary reflector oven, make a frame-work using wire coat hangers, skewers, or what-ever works; then enclose an oven-like space with aluminum foil, opened to the fire side.

Baking can also be done in a square, folding oven that sits on top of a camp stove or over a fire. Baking takes longer than in a normal oven, but any fresh-baked bread or dessert tastes wonderful when you're camping. The oven collapses into a flat package for transport.

Easiest of all portable ovens is a large roasting bag, or a length of roasting wrap or aluminum foil, placed over any makeshift framework to confine heat. Keep heat low, to achieve more even cooking without bottom-burning.

There are also "Outback" ovens in the shape of a deep frying pan, designed for use with camp stoves, in which you can "bake" pizzas, breads, or cakes.

# CAMP KITCHEN

## 14

It's fairly easy to think minimal when you're choosing clothes for a weekend outdoors; but when you start packing cooking equipment, it's hard to know what to eliminate. When you set up substitute housekeeping, certain things seem essential, whether you plan to be away for two days or two months.

You *could* stick to cold cereal, sandwiches, and finger-food dinners from the grill; then you don't need pots, pans, or plates. That's actually fun for a couple of weekends, but eventually you want to fix other foods. Car campers can bring almost as much kitchen stuff as they'd like, initially taken straight from cabinet to car; when packing for a canoe trip, you may need to be a bit more conservative.

When camping becomes a regular thing, it's practical to have a "camping only" inventory of pots, utensils, and dishes. Head for the camping store, browse the garage sales, or shop a local flea market.

## COOKING POTS

The Dutch oven could be your ticket to one-pot camping. For entrees you have the option of stewing, roasting, or frying; you can cook meats and vegetables together in a sauce, or separated by foil wraps, even though it all cooks in the same pot. Use the Dutch oven for baking, too: prop cake or muffin tins on a few small rocks placed in the bottom of the oven (or on an upside-down cake pan) for even baking without bottom-burning. (A pressure cooker could achieve many of the same results—and then some.)

"Real" camping pots are different from home pots. The most significant difference is that camp-ing pots are more likely to have bucket-type bail handles so they can hang over a campfire. Camping pots are often sold in sets of graduated sizes; handles either come off or fold in, so pots nest completely into one another for the most compact storage. Some camp cookware is designed without handles, to nest compactly; you use a metal *pot lifter* to grip the edge of the pot.

With some camp cookware, a lid becomes a frying pan—you just invert it and attach a handle or use a pot lifter.

Camping cook sets are made of aluminum—some with non-stick interiors—or stainless steel. Most cooks already have a preferred material.

Home pots can nest, too—they just do it on a tilt because the handles don't come off (see illustration, next page). When packing them, finish the nest with a coffee mug cushioned by a dish towel. No point in wasting space.

Besides some nesting saucepans, bring one or two frying pans (covers aren't essential; you can always use aluminum foil). If you'll be cooking on a two-burner camp stove, think about a long griddle. It covers both burners, and holds a bunch of pancakes or burgers. Plus, you can play short-order cook with bacon, eggs, and hash browns.

Propped over a wood or charcoal fire, a hinged, double-sided pan-on-a-stick cooks a burger, meat pie, hot sandwich, or dessert mini-pie. Buy cast iron, or Teflon-coated aluminum, depending on whether you're a traditionalist or a true believer in easy cleaning. Called a sandwich cooker or pie iron, they're sold at camping stores.

The home kitchen's Teflon omelet pan works for camp cooking, too, allowing you to cook larger (if strangely shaped) sandwiches or pies.

If you have plenty of room to tote extras, a campfire popcorn popper is a good one; popcorn's a universally loved snack.

A two-sided broiler basket with a long handle lets you control the heat (by controlling the height) when cooking ground meat or fish, grilled sandwiches, or toast.

# COOKING HELPS

Any number of "stick" variations can be used for cooking over a fire. One giant fork holds six hot dogs at once. Choose smaller forks or skewers for traditional marshmallow toasting, which must be done by the individual "to-taste" method. (Not everyone appreciates charmallows.)

Long-handled forks, tongs, and spatulas are necessary. Look for those with non-heat-conducting handles, and keep a pair of thermal quilted elbow-length mitts for insurance.

For easy carrying and convenient using, put cloth pockets onto a canvas backing, one for each of your cooking utensils—spatula, stirring spoon, big fork, whatever you normally use. When cooking, unroll the holder so everything is reachable. To carry and store, roll it up and tie it shut.

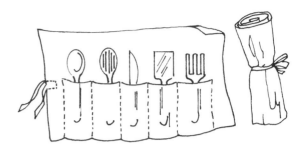

*Cloth pockets on a canvas backing.*

Other essential utensils: Get a good plastic cutting board (thinner, lighter-weight, easier to sanitize than wood), and don't forget a mechanical can opener. Many households don't own a hand-powered can opener anymore; buy a good one, or you'll be sorry (Swing-A-Way is a kitchen classic). Another item you may not find in the kitchen junk drawer is an old-fashioned can and bottle opener; you may need one. Also think about a corkscrew, if you like to enjoy wine with dinner.

See pages 143–44 for a checklist of food preparation items.

Take paper towels for napkins as well as mop-up, plus assorted types of plastic bags, for leftovers, trash, and miscellaneous storage. Bring plenty of matches, for the fire, stove, lantern, candles.

# DINING WARE

Campers go through a lot of paper plates (*not* foam—they won't burn cleanly in the fire when you're done), but some meals require a more solid base. Take plastic dinner plates, plus medium-size bowls to use for soup, salad, cereal, or chili.

Disposable plastic glasses can be used many times before they crack; paper cups can be burned. Your choice, for these and for the paper plates, depends a lot on a personal tree-saving philosophy.

Coffee, cocoa, bouillon, and tea all taste better from a ceramic mug than from a plastic cup. Breakage is a minor problem; you can always replace a mug if it chips too badly.

Take enough silverware so you won't have to wash dinner forks before you can serve dessert pie. Add a couple of sharp knives (large, small, serrated,

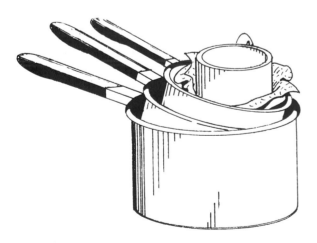

*Nest as many items as possible to utilize space (add a salt shaker inside the cup).*

# Cookware

- Take a coffee pot only if fresh-brewed coffee is a necessity for your family. Otherwise, any pot can heat water to use with tea or coffee bags, or to steep loose tea or ground coffee through filter funnels. For a special occasion surprise, a non-electric mini espresso maker can tuck into a tiny corner to add a classy finish to a camp supper.
- Forget the pots; heat canned foods in their cans. Open the top, but don't remove it completely; bend it up enough to allow steam to escape and a stir-spoon to enter, and set the can on the stove, grill, or over the campfire.
- Use a pot-holding gadget (pot lifter) to handle the hot can. Pliers would do it, but the pot lifter holds the can at a better angle.
- If you need a rolling pin, use a can or bottle. Cut biscuits or shape hamburger patties with a can. Improvise wherever you can.
- For kabob cooking, use skewers made from twisted metal. Round skewers may spin around inside the food.
- A toaster designed for campfire use resembles a metal pyramid. It holds four slices, but it takes

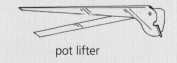

pot lifter

practice to use; bread may dry out or char. To toast in a frying pan, use a non-stick pan, and don't add any cooking oil. Or, spear the bread with a fork and toast like a marshmallow.
- Use a frying pan on a stove or fire to bake biscuits, muffins, small cakes. Grease the bottom and dust with flour, to prevent burning.
- Use a large coffee can (with top and bottom removed) to quick-bake banana bread or corn-bread.
- Disposable foil baking pans find many uses around camp. Use one upside down for a lid, if your cookpot doesn't have one. Set one rightside up on top of the cookpot, and heat dinner rolls. Clip two together with clothespins (top over bottom) and use as a warming oven for rolls or garlic bread. (Set away from flame, at side of fire.)
- Nest-pack your dishes, too: mixing bowl, cereal bowls, and a glass or cup inside the top bowl.
- Bring a quart bottle or covered pitcher to mix juice from frozen or other concentrate refills. Use the larger-size juice mix, then pour servings of half juice from bottle, half water. (Saves space in the cooler, but juice will still be cool.)
- Bring a measuring cup only if you have trouble estimating proper amounts with a drinking glass or coffee mug.
- Bring a set of straw plate holders;

they help to prevent lap spills caused by weak or wet paper plates.
- Bring a bunch of twist ties. If you always run out at home, too, buy a whole roll of the coated wire at the camping store. Buy a bright color so you can retrieve those that hit the dust.
- Keep flying bugs out of soft-drink cans. Plastic lids cover the pop-top portion of the can with plastic bars that block all but the smallest flying drink-stealers.
- When you're in a camping store, look for the flip-top lids that cap film canisters to recycle them into salt and pepper shakers. (A few grains of rice kept inside will help to absorb the dampness of outdoor living.) The lids work with Kodak film holders.
- Old prescription bottles work well for spices.
- Pack muffin, cornbread, pancake, or other premeasured mixes in zip-top bags. When you're ready to cook, add liquid ingredients and use the sealed bag as a mixing bowl. (Write directions on the bag, if necessary.)
- Buy (or make) little cheesecloth tents to cover food—keeps bugs away.

cheesecloth tent

straight), a potato peeler, a cheese grater, any kitchen gadgets you use a lot. They don't take much space.

When you're not using pots for cooking, they're

good mixing and serving bowls; bring a few disposable foil pans for assorted uses. Buy the extra-large roll of heavy-duty aluminum foil; besides using it for cooking, you can shape a bowl for chips

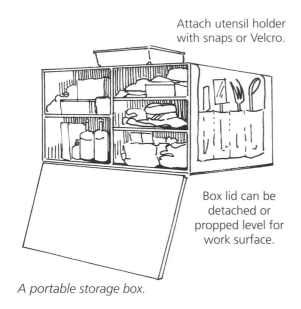

Attach utensil holder with snaps or Velcro.

Box lid can be detached or propped level for work surface.

*A portable storage box.*

or a basket for bread. Then recycle the foil for next night's dinner.

# PORTABLE ORGANIZERS

Anything that helps to organize the kitchen area is good, whether it's a divided packing box, a few plastic milk crates, or an entire portable unit—a counter-and-cabinet arrangement that folds up and out to hold a whole miniature kitchen. Personal experience suggests simpler is better, but whichever you choose, it's most helpful when things are visible (at least, after lifting one lid), so no searching or rummaging is necessary. Visibility not only prevents the constant "where" queries, but it helps your camping companions help themselves.

Use ¼-inch plywood to make a storage box for kitchen items and divide it into whatever size and number of compartments you want.

Some families find such a box most useful as a snack stand: paper plates, paper towels for napkins, eating utensils, crackers and cheese, peanut butter and jelly, trail mix, dried fruit, sandwich condiments. This has the added advantage of establishing which foods are meant for snacks, and which are to be kept for a pre-planned meal.

Other campers keep the portable cabinet as the cooking station: foil, plastic wrap, food bags, cutting board, knives, cooking oil, spices, sauces. Whoever is cook for the day can find what they need to work with.

Once you establish what each section should hold, it's also obvious what to add to the buy list when a vacancy occurs.

In transit, the box sits on its side with the hinged opening front panel on top, holding its compartmentalized contents securely in place. When set up for use, the hinged panel folds down out of the way, or can be propped level to use as a shelf or countertop (if so, cover it with plastic laminate).

# CRUNCH KEEPERS

Dry foods usually go camping in one of two ways: either use a collection of same-size, screw-top plastic containers (for breakfast cereal, crackers, and whatever dry staples you need for each trip's menu), or put all of the above into zip-top plastic bags. The idea is to get rid of excess packaging while retaining "dry" character. With the reusable plastic containers, you have a little extra protection from crumbling without adding more plastic to the landfill (though some campers wash and reuse the heavier plastic bags, canceling that objection). The bag method takes the least space, so if that's a consideration, the choice is made. The obvious third possibility is to leave everything in original boxes, which you burn when empty. This works for campers with large vans, and where campfires are allowed. It does not work well on hot and humid days, when dry foods act like sponges. (If your crackers lose their crunch, toss them in a frying pan and heat gently for a few minutes.)

# SAFE KEEPERS

Egg cartons made of plastic are a sensible extra; eggs will be safer in the plastic than in the store's paper or Styrofoam.

Buy reusable squeeze tubes for jams, mustard, catsup, relish, and mayonnaise. Neater serving, they're also safer keeping: no air or foreign particles can get to the food. (Buy the tubes from camping supply stores or catalogs.)

## Cool (and Hot) Stuff

- Block ice lasts longest; next best is cubes. Don't buy flaked or crushed unless you have no choice; it will soon be slush.
- Prepare meals at home and freeze them in boiling-safe plastic bags. At camp, heat the bag in boiling water, and shorten cleanup efforts.
- Zip-top bags are good for cooler storage of salad, vegetables, or leftovers; they scrunch up to fit available spaces.
- Insulated jugs—some with pour spouts—are convenient for iced tea and other cold drinks when you have ample water supply to rinse them well.

- Not essential, but welcome: insulated foam holders keep individual soda cans cool long enough for even slow drinkers.
- When the campground is within a two-hour drive, fix the first night's dinner at home. Keep it hot in a heavy pot (your Dutch oven?) wrapped in several layers of newspaper or placed in a cardboard box—or in a Styrofoam cooler, a thermal tote bag, or a 12-volt hot-or-cold keeper.
- Described as thermoelectric, the cooler-shaped portable Koolatron refrigerator can operate in heat mode as well, but if you use

it to keep your pre-cooked dinner warm on the way to camp, don't plan on using it as a cooler immediately after dinner, as it takes some time to cool down to refrigeration temperature. (Check manufacturer's recommendations.)
- Wherever ice cream cakes are sold, the store packs them in insulated bags for the trip home. These bags keep the ice cream frozen; they can also keep food warm. (Dairy Queen sells them for about $4.)

# COLD KEEPERS

As basic as cooler technology would seem to be, manufacturers continue to devise improvements—or at least new features. You can choose a cooler with a hinged lid or a loose lid; the latter can be flipped over to use as a serving table surface. You can buy hard plastic coolers (to sit on) or soft thermal fabric (to fold away when not being used). Some coolers have a top food tray where perishables like lettuce or sprouts can be kept away from the ice. The tray also eliminates the likelihood of sopping-wet sandwiches. Some handles tuck into side indentations, out of the way until needed for carrying.

One practical cooler has the mobility of a wagon, with a pull handle on one end and two wheels on the other.

For useful features, how about a cooler with a built-in light, just like the home fridge? It's battery operated, and a switch ensures that you won't waste the battery during daylight hours—assuming you remember to use the switch.

## Pre-cool

Reusable blue plastic freezer packs work as intended, but if you freeze water (or lemonade or

other fruit drinks) in plastic bottles, you'll have ice to start the camping trip, and cool drinking water (or drinks) as it melts. Don't fill containers completely; allow space for freezer expansion. For the cooling benefit, and to save at-camp cooking time, prepare and pre-freeze food items, too: chili, meat loaf, pasta sauces.

When packing the cooler, pre-chill everything (including the cooler itself: toss in a few ice cubes). Frozen food or ice stays as close to the top as practical, since cold travels down. Put the cooler in the car, if at all possible; the trunk gets too hot. Wrap the cooler in cardboard, a blanket, or some other insulator, and the ice will last even longer.

At camp, keep the cooler in the shade so the ice can do its job as long as possible. Leave melted water inside as long as it stays cold; a filled cooler retains cold better than empty air space. (Larger coolers have drain plugs so you can easily control the amount of ice water you want to keep inside, releasing only enough so contents are not afloat.)

If space permits, use two coolers, one for beverages and snacks (this will be opened often) and one for the food to be kept cold for mealtime (less opening, longer cold-keeping). This also lessens the chances of the food cooler being left open a crack.

## Super-Chill

If taking meat for a week's trip, dry ice will keep it best. Wrap the dry ice in layers of newspaper and place it on top of your pre-frozen meat packages. Don't let the dry ice come into direct contact with the cooler, or it could warp the plastic. As long as it's well wrapped, it's okay to use.

## Real Refrigeration

At campgrounds with electric outlets at each tent site, you could have another way to keep food cold. Cooler-sized and -shaped portable refrigerators can be operated on 12-volt DC or 120-volt AC. As you drive to camp, connect it to the car's 12-volt system (cigarette lighter plug-in); at camp, switch to the 120-volt cord. You won't have a separate freezer compartment, and it may not hold as much food as a comparable-size cooler, since some interior space is taken by the cooling mechanism and the walls are thicker for insulating. Still, it is definitely a more consistent cold than ice provides.

When you plan to use it for the weekend, plug it into house power the night before you leave, to pre-chill it, too, as you would a regular cooler.

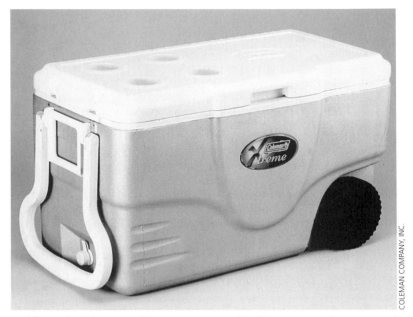

COLEMAN COMPANY, INC.

*Adding wheels to a cooler—a true example of how necessity prompted invention.*

# WATER FAUCETS

At most commercial campgrounds, you'll probably be able to attach a water hose at your tent site and leave it there, so that water is handy whenever you need it.

So-called wilderness camping areas have different levels of amenities. Some have water available at a few central sites. Some have no improvements; your water source is the nearest stream, river, or lake.

For those places where you'll be ferrying water, whether from a tap at the bathhouse or from a natural water source, bring easily carried jerry jugs, preferably 3-gallon square or rectangular bottles (the 5-gallon size is too heavy for most people when full). If you don't have room to pack these, two kinds of collapsible bottles can be used: either the sides fold in to make a narrow package when empty, or a not-quite-accordion type folds down as flat as you can squash it (see page 109). Canvas buckets (find them in marine stores, if not elsewhere) are another space-saving option.

For weekend trips (and always assuming the vehicle has space), many campers bring drinking water from home, even if the campground has water at each site. Whether it's bottled water from the supermarket or your own carry jug filled from the home faucet, the home water may be what it takes to encourage everybody to drink the water they need. Water from different locations can be surprisingly different in taste. City dwellers may not find chlorine objectionable, and country gentlepersons are familiar with iron, but vice versa and nobody's happy.

The supermarket's 2½-gallon bottle of drinking water is handy for its turn-handle spout; set it up on a stump or rock, and even small children can get their own water without trying to lift a heavy jug or open a cooler umpteen unnecessary times a day.

Another way to encourage everyone to drink more water is to squeeze a hint of lime juice into a

# Washing Up

- Some campers suggest it's not necessary to use hot water for dishes unless your food was especially fatty. But besides cutting grease, hot water also sanitizes, preventing any growth of food-borne bacteria.
- When you're through cooking, start heating a large pot of water for dishes. It will be ready when you've finished eating.
- If you have a teakettle, use it to give dishes a hot-water rinse.
- To ease cleanup when cooking over a fire, coat the outside of pots with liquid dish soap, or a paste of bar soap and water; black soot will wash off more easily.
- After grill cooking, remove the grill from the heat and set it onto wet newspapers—or cover it with wet paper towels. The steaming softens burned-on food particles.
- To avoid all-day glass-washing, get a different color plastic glass for each person. If campers want to rinse their glass between orange juice and lemonade, they can—themselves.
- A small grab bracket with suction cups on the back side attaches wherever you need it. A half sponge fits inside, and dries out between uses.
- You can buy a small, portable sink to use for dishwashing. Rinse water is inside a built-in tank. Run a drain hose to the bucket. Another type of portable sink inflates for use, deflates for packing.
- Use a piece of 4-mil sheet plastic nested among logs and rocks to hold it in the shape of a sink.
- Dilute your dish soap (one part soap to two parts water, if it's a very sudsy brand) to avoid excessive rinsing.
- Put the dishcloth and the dish-drying towel in the sun every day to dry thoroughly.

**Camp Rule #1:** Whoever cooks, doesn't do dishes.

portable sink

gallon bottle. It's not enough to really taste like lime, but it does something to make the water taste more fresh and refreshing.

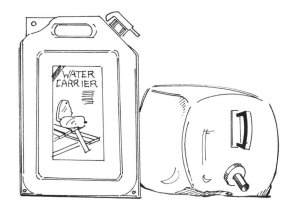

*Collapsible water carriers can either "fold" into a fairly flat rectangle (left) or collapse to fit into a smaller space (right).*

# WATER SOURCES

Once upon a time, you could dip water from a wilderness stream and drink it safely, but those times and places are mostly gone. You'll still find the occasional spring where water runs pure, and is often checked by local testing agencies. In most places, if you're using found water for drinking, cooking, or dishes, you must first treat it in some way to make it safe.

## Heat

Boiling is still a reliable way to kill germs, including *E. coli* bacteria and *Giardia lamblia*. The most cautious time recommendation is now 20 minutes. Boiling, of course, takes time and uses stove fuel. Some people don't like the taste of boiled water; others can't *find* a taste. If your water source happens to have a lot of tea-colored tannic acid, boiling won't make it *look* any more appetizing.

# Water

- White water hoses (bought at camping or marine stores) are good because they don't add any noticeable flavor to the water running through them.
- A 25-foot length of hose is usually plenty; the tap will either be at the individual campsite, or it won't, and if not, you don't need the hose at all.
- Put a small filter on the hose; it helps remove any unpleasant taste caused by plumbing pipes,

a filter on a hose

or whatever special component might be found in the local water supply that is both unfamiliar and unwelcome.

- If you buy drinking water, look for refill machines at supermarkets. Save money, save recycling the bottles.
- When you do buy water, look for screw-on tops rather than pop-off, so you can reuse the bottles without worrying about spills.
- When water's plentiful, a solar still is an interesting show-and-tell project for the children. Someday, if water's not available, it might be a significant part of survival.

To make a solar still, you must dig a hole. In a real survival situation, it should be about 3 feet in diameter; for demonstration, think miniature. Choose a

place with sandy soil, to imitate the desert conditions that might prompt use of the still. Place a tin can at the bottom center of the hole, and cover all with a piece of plastic. Put a few stones over the plastic around the edge of the hole so the plastic doesn't fall in, and place one stone in the middle of the plastic to weigh it down over the can beneath. When the sun warms the area, moisture from the sand will evaporate, hit the plastic, condense to liquid, and drain along the sagging plastic to drip into the can.

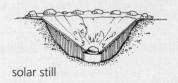

solar still

## Additives

It's fairly common knowledge that some form of chlorine is used to purify water—just taste any city water supply. And, it's been common practice for years that individuals have used a bit of chlorine bleach to disinfect questionable water; but, since water purification is not the business of a bleach company, you won't find instructions on the label. (If bleach is all you have, use 8 drops per gallon.)

It's probably better to use water purification tablets; they're made for their special purpose. Most use iodine to treat the water. While noses turn up at the mention of iodine, the manufacturer of one such product—Potable Aqua—uses a second additive, P.A. Plus, to take away the bad taste.

"Common knowledge" also says, "Don't use iodine tablets for a long time," but the definition of "long" varies from a few days to six weeks. If you have concerns, ask your pharmacist or doctor.

## Portable Filters

Small, water-filtering pumps (like Katadyn, PUR, and First Need) provide another way to purify water, removing bacteria like *E. coli* and *Salmonella,* and protozoa (cysts, sometimes called parasites) like *Giardia lamblia.* Some filters also screen out chemicals from runoff; others can remove viruses, though this is not a major concern in the United States or Canada.

Without some kind of water treatment—either boiling, purification tablets, or filter—you risk severe stomach cramps, vomiting, and diarrhea that can lead to dehydration.

# WATER USAGE

Kitchen chores require some special attention to water usage and disposal.

Washing dishes is never fun; that doesn't change much at camp. Do it as quickly as possible with a simple substitute sink/drainer/drain arrangement.

First rule: Dirty dishwater (gray water) does not drain onto the ground; use a bucket to collect it. At commercial campgrounds, empty the bucket into the appropriately named "slop sink," usually outside the bathhouse. In the wilderness, scatter it away from the tent site, where it can filter naturally through sand or soil. (Some suggest digging a hole, and pouring the gray water into it.)

To do dishes, use a stainless steel bowl, or a rectangular plastic box for the hot dishwater. Dip a sponge or cloth into the soapy water, and wash everything. Stack sudsy dishes on paper towels or a plastic bag. Rinse everything over the bucket (hold dish in one hand, pour water from a 2-liter soda bottle with the other), and stack in a dish pan to drain.

If you wipe plates and pots with paper towels before washing, they'll clean up easier. Also, if you spin or shake the cups and glasses as you're pouring water, they'll rinse faster. To pack up, nest the dish soap, sponge, and washing bowl inside the dish pan; put the 2-liter bottle inside the bucket.

In wilderness camping areas, it's especially important to use the right soaps. Buy the mildest, natural, non-polluting, biodegradable products you can find, to keep contaminants out of the water source that ultimately catches your dishwater. You can follow Jacques Cousteau's lead and use Shaklee products; look in the business white pages of your local phone directory for a distributor in your area.

*Backpackers and canoeists sometimes must find and filter drinking water.*

# OUTDOOR LORE

## 15

It's a given that campers like the outdoors—the more they explore, the more they want to see. Even campgrounds with all the resort amenities often save a corner of their land for a small nature trail, perhaps with labels identifying plants and a display of photographs showing wildlife that was once indigenous. Many government lands are expanded nature trails, providing miles of forest, dune, or meadow to explore.

The best way to see nature's wonders, whether your particular focus is wildflowers, nesting birds, or swamp frogs, is to walk among them. Wandering through a wilderness setting, you wait for the chance meetings when a bird, bug, or animal allows a glimpse into its world. Walking puts you as close as you'll get to being eye-to-eye with nature. You'll experience the thrill of discovery that comes with the simplest things: finding a seed pod from your favorite wildflower; hearing an unfamiliar bird call; following a line of paw prints till they fade into the forest floor.

Watching children make their own private discoveries doubles the enjoyment for you. Children see things with a perspective many adults have lost. They question everything, forcing thought even when answers are slow to come. When exploring nature becomes the highlight of a day, then shopping malls and TV shows and video screens are put on back memory; that in itself is a success of camping.

## TAKE A HIKE

If the word *hiking* conjures a boot-shod backpacker climbing a rugged mountain trail, then think "stroll through the country" instead, because that's what most campers do; hiking is simply the means to whatever ends are found on the path to the other side of the hill.

Make a rough estimate of the area you want to cover, remembering that distances shown on a map correspond to how far a bird will travel; *you* will be spending time and energy on up-and-down routes as well, and trails always seem to curve more than map representations show. Plan your hikes around the physical condition of the youngest or weakest walker; this should be fun, not a physical challenge. The younger the children, the shorter the hike; while children generally like to walk, they do get sidetracked easily and often. Take snacks, some juice boxes, and plenty of water. Bring a few plastic bags for important keepers like the hollow beetle body discovered by the observant three-year-old.

With infants, a stroller is obviously impractical on a forest trail. Mom may start out with baby in a front carrier, then Dad takes over with baby in a backpack. Parents split the time carrying the extra weight, and baby enjoys the rides and the views.

Only long-distance hikers need real hiking boots, but sturdy shoes are better than sneakers for feet, legs, and back. Ankle-high styles will give even more support; also make sure the soles have a good tread and will keep a grip on the trail. Whatever footgear you wear, it should be broken in.

Hikers often wear two pairs of socks, for the cushioning effect, but unless you wore this combination when you bought your shoes or boots, they won't fit comfortably with the added thickness. You can buy "sport-specific" styles of acrylic socks,

*A section of a topographic map.*

Sample legend:

═══════ primary highway (red)

▬▬▬▬▬ secondary highway (red and white)

- - - - trail

╫ bridge

╫Ⓞ╫ drawbridge

╫╪╪╫ tunnel

┼┼┼ railroad (standard gauge, single track)

▬ ▨ buildings

✕ airport

● ◙ tanks

△ campground

⋉ picnic tables

⟍•⟋ power transmission line, pole, tower

‒‒‒‒‒ telephone/under-ground pipeline

⟋⟨ mine tunnel

⤫ gravel, sand pit

or you can wear thick cotton or wool socks and take along some Band-Aids or moleskin to discourage any blisters from starting.

# MAP READING

Most family camping is done in areas with marked trails where a compass isn't necessary. But any outdoor hike is ideal for studying map information and relating it to compass use. The maps commonly used for land navigation are *topographic maps*, which add a third dimension to directional informa-

tion, showing the height and shape of the land by using *contour lines*.

All points on one contour line are the same level, or elevation. A perfectly shaped hill would be drawn in a series of circular contour lines. So would a perfectly rounded dip, but checking the elevation figures would show whether the cone shape went up or down.

On American and Canadian maps, color also helps provide information quickly. Contour lines are brown, water areas are blue, forests green. Important roads are indicated in red; other roads and

*It's very rewarding (and useful) to find your way by using compass (here, a Silva) and map.*

man-made features like tanks, buildings, and power lines are black. The color or character of a line or shape is explained in a *legend* that is part of each "topo" map.

# SIMPLE NAVIGATION

A map can provide a compass heading from A to B, but instead of trying to follow a course given in degrees, most campers navigate by locating landmarks along the course, then walking landmark-to-landmark.

To find a direction to travel and a landmark to follow, you should first position the map so *its* north matches the land's north. With a lot of easily recognized landmarks, you can do this visually: for example, when the map's mountain peak symbol faces the real mountain, and the radio tower mark is on a line with the real tower, you've *oriented* the map to the land. Now pencil a line from where you are to where you want to go. Look for a map landmark along that line that you can also identify on the ground, and go for it. When you get there, look again, and walk again. Not very sophis-

ticated, but it works for most day hikers—except perhaps in dense fog or white-out snow, conditions the summer camper is unlikely to find.

Of course, it is possible to orient the map more scientifically, with an *orienteering compass*: a combination protractor, compass, and distance scale that lets you plot a bearing from a map, find your *heading* (direction of travel) in the field, and take checkpoint bearings from landmarks along the way.

# ANIMAL ALERT

When children or adults first see the indentation in the soil as a hoof mark or paw print, it's no small thrill to realize you're walking the same path as a moose or a raccoon. (One nephew could hardly believe he was sharing territory with a "real" mink.) Know what you're looking for, and be prepared to identify what you find. When you set off on a hike, bring along one or more field guides (nature reference books) about the animals you'll find in the area, showing prints and droppings, and describing food and habits.

# Walking Tips

- Many variables affect walking time, but start by guessing you can walk a mile of easy trail (level and rockless) in about a half hour. Double the guess for difficult terrain, add more when carrying a child or pack. Don't forget to allow time for rest and lunch stops.
- Whenever you walk, make mental notes of the path for the return trip (look behind you as well as ahead) and to heighten your own observation ability.
- Some campers like to use a walking stick, or hiking staff. It's good on a long hike, and on up-and-down trails, especially for campers with knee problems. It helps hikers keep their balance when crossing streams, especially with a pack.
- Tuck some Band-Aids in your pocket; if a shoe or boot rubs wrong, you can cushion the spot before you get a blister.
- If you're caught outdoors in a thunderstorm, lightning is your worst worry. It should be common knowledge to avoid places lightning might hit (single tall trees), yet people continue to seek shelter in just those places. If you're in an open area, kneel on the ground and lower your head to make yourself as low as possible. Keep ground contact as small as possible. If you seek shelter in a cave, go inside; don't stay near the entrance. To estimate distance between you and a storm, count the seconds between lightning and thunder. Divide by five, and you'll know the approximate number of miles away.

# Search Tips

- If you're in a situation where a plane might be involved in a search, make an X or SOS pattern on the ground in a clearing, using logs or rocks, to signal the pilot. Also, lay out any bright-colored clothing flat on the ground, to catch a pilot's eye.
- Even if you don't have a compass, you can find north: Place a stick straight down into the ground and mark the end of its shadow at 10:00 A.M. (sun time) and again at 2:00 P.M.—or at other times that are equal hours away from noon. Measure the distance between marks, and divide in half; a line from the stick to the halfway mark points to true north. If you don't have a watch, mark the end of the first shadow at estimated mid-morning. As the sun moves over the stick, the shadow will be cast from the opposite direction. When the second shadow is the same length as the first, mark its end, and find north the same way as above.
- File a float plan or travel plan with a responsible person; indicate where you plan to go and when you expect to return.
- Put bright-colored clothes on the children. Establish a buddy system when backcountry camping with kids; nobody goes anywhere alone.

# Survival Tips

- The most familiar edible wild plants are dandelions and clover (leaves and flowers) and cattails (shoots, stalks, roots, and the tops before yellow pollen appears).
- If you need to forage, first test plant edibility: Rub juice from the plant on your lips to see if you experience any bad reaction. If not, start eating small amounts of the leaves. Don't eat milky-stemmed plants, except dandelions. If you have water and fire, boil leaves before eating.
- When choosing plants to eat, try to see what the resident wildlife eat (rabbits, raccoons, squirrels, even bears). Don't follow a bird's lead. The inner bark of many trees is edible: poplar, red maple, birch, willow, and most pine. Try evergreen needles, acorns, and other nuts and seeds, including those in pinecones.
- Wild blueberries and blackberries will be a treat. (Don't eat any white berries.) At the seashore, look for clams, mussels, oysters, fish (if you can catch one), or seaweed (gather only the fresh seaweed still in the water, not on the beach).

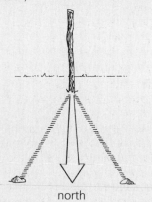

north

## Compass Tips

- Orienteering compasses may print the two most commonly used map scales on the *base-plate*, so you can read distances directly, without referring to the map's printed legend. Some have a built-in magnifying glass, some a *clinometer* to measure slope.
- Memorize degree numbers of cardinal directions to help prevent an "opposite" error—a common mistake of neglecting to mentally reverse a bearing that you read. North is 0 degrees, east 90, south 180, and west 270.
- If you see the term "grid north" on a topo map, ignore it. It may be significant to mapmakers, but not to hikers/campers.
- Instead of trying to stay on a particular compass course, many experienced hikers look for a road or power line running roughly parallel to their course, and follow *it* till a turn to right or left brings them to their objective.
- Identify two landmarks on map and trail, preferably about 90 degrees apart. With a compass, take bearings on each; draw

cross bearings

pencil lines from the landmarks along the reciprocal (reverse) bearing. The place where the two lines cross is your position.
- For information or topo maps:

Map Distribution
U.S. Geological Survey Information Services (topographic maps)
P.O. Box 25287
Denver, CO 80225
888-ASK-USGS (888-275-8747)
http://ask.usgs.gov/

In Canada:
Canada Map Office
Dept. of Energy, Mines, and Resources

615 Booth Street
Ottawa, Ontario
K1A 0E9, Canada
800-465-6277
http://maps.nrcan.gc.ca/cmo/dealers.html

- Trails Illustrated prints enhanced versions of USGS maps on plastic (so waterproof). These include additional information on the area as a guide to trip planning. Call 800-962-1643.

ground configuration shown by contour lines

Teach the children to "think quiet"; practice walking to blend in with natural sounds of forest or marsh. Practice looking, to seek out what would otherwise be invisible; be aware of each animal's natural camouflage, and try to distinguish resident wildlife from their background cover. Watch for the small, quick motions that might give away a hiding place. Practice listening, to isolate a sound and give it identity.

Watch for animals early in the day and again at dusk; they're more active at those times. Once you do spot a wild animal, don't try to get close; you'll probably just alert the animal, and it will run. Never offer animals food; they could become dependent on such handouts, and they might also become aggressive.

# EMERGENCY

Weekend and vacation campers probably don't need to know survival techniques; they won't likely be scaling sheer cliffs or mapping unexplored caves. But the outdoors is a good place to learn something about self-sufficiency in the wilderness, and it doesn't hurt to know "lost" signals and how to go about finding yourself or a lost camper.

"Lost" is the start of many outdoor emergencies. You forget to note a turn while hiking, or an overturned canoe gets away from you. You may have some survival gear with you, or you may have nothing at all. A word to the wise for outdoor folks: Find room for a small emergency kit, and wear it on

a belt or in a fanny pack. If nothing else, pin whistles to everyone's jacket whenever you're in backcountry areas.

## Lost Hiker

If you have map and compass, but are confused about your location, try to reorient yourself. Climb a tree, or walk to a hilltop for a longer overview; maybe you'll spot a creek or a power line—anything to use as a baseline back to familiar territory.

If nothing matches your map from this perspective, make a plan to look for identifiable landmarks. You should stay in the general area where you first realized you were lost; plot search patterns from there (see below). With "X" as your center, walk out a specified distance (or time) in each of the cardinal directions, always returning to "X." If nothing looks familiar, start walking a square half-mile or mile; then try a "growing square," keeping track of all time and turns so you can always return to "X."

## Lost Camper

If you're a lost camper of stranded canoeist *without* a compass, try not to panic; most lost people in the United States are found very quickly. Stay put; don't try to "find" yourself if you haven't any real leads, or you may wander farther away from the place where someone last saw you. Canoeists should stay near the water; that's where the searchers will look.

Start signaling, with a whistle or mirror, even shouts if that's your only option. Signal three times, pause 10 seconds; three more times, pause, and so on.

If you can start a fire, do so, for signaling (smoke) and for your own comfort and peace of mind (for warmth and to deter animals and insects). A survival kit will have waterproof matches or other means to start a fire. The science lesson about flint and steel making sparks comes in handy here; a pocket knife struck against an ordinary rock may work, too. People have started fires by directing a sunbeam through glass (binoculars, eyeglass lens, or magnifying glass) and also with friction, as in rubbing two sticks together.

In rainy weather, dry tinder will be hard to find. Look under rock overhangs, and at the base of trees with a dense canopy. Birchbark makes good tinder, or use bits of clothing or cotton from a first-aid kit.

Think about shelter. If you have the survival kit, use the emergency ("space") blanket for a lean-to; otherwise, make up a windbreak shelter from branches, bark, whatever. In mountains, look for caves and overhangs, but stay away from them in thunderstorms.

Look for water. People can get along for three weeks or more without food, but only a few days without water. With the survival kit will be water purification tablets. If you haven't a kit, perhaps you could boil the water in a canteen (assuming you are able to start a fire and have a canteen with you).

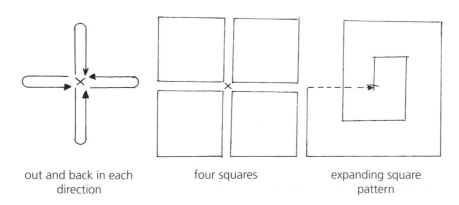

out and back in each direction

four squares

expanding square pattern

*Search patterns can help you reorient yourself.*

## Searchers

If someone in your group is lost, establish where the person was last seen, and station someone there to set up continuous signals. It's usually recommended that you seek professional help for a search, which will benefit from local knowledge and access to all available assistance.

The following list offers some suggestions for a survival kit (optional items are in parentheses).

*Signaling:* Whistle, mirror, (smoke flares)

*Firemaking/light:* Waterproof matches, metal match with steel wool, candle stub, commercial fire-starting sticks, (lightsticks)

*Shelter:* Space blanket, wire saw, monofilament or other line, knife, (multi-use tool)

*Navigation:* Backup compass

*First aid:* Aspirin, Band-Aids, antiseptic, tweezers, (snakebite kit)

*Food/water:* Water purification tablets, polyethylene sheet, bouillon, small metal tackle box with monofilament line, fish hooks, sinkers, (canteen)

*Manual of survival tips*

# OUTDOOR FUN

## 16

Since camping itself is intended for enjoyment, it seems redundant to center a whole chapter around ways to have fun. But after the busywork of setting up camp is done, there is free time to fill, and it seems appropriate to fill it in a way that is productive as well as fun. Not that you can't leave some hours of the day for relaxing and recharging the batteries of body and mind, but your time outdoors is usually so precious you don't want to let too much slip away; you'd like to explore as much of your surroundings as you can.

Whatever you do, let the surroundings be your focus. If you like to read, get a book on the habitat or history of the area; even novels are written with a strong sense of place. If you're a true history buff, your whole camp can be a living history display—reliving ways of the past, like those groups that revert to Elizabethan, Renaissance, or Civil War times, just for the weekend. If you're after photo opportunities, just aim: everywhere you turn will be a picture waiting to be framed. If you're seeking tranquility, take a small boat for a few hours of absolute escapism.

No matter how you choose to fill your time, any marked change from your usual routine will bring a dual benefit: it can lower your stress level and increase your sense of well-being.

## BOATING

Many camping areas have some kind of water on-site or nearby—duck pond, stream or river, inland lake or coastal shoreline—none of which can be truly explored without a boat. It's not difficult to

*A PortaBote rows easily, or can be pushed by a small outboard. It folds to a 4-inch flat package to tie on a car.*

# Boat Tips

- An aluminum canoe or rowboat could scratch your car, so have a good mounting setup and system. Simple foam blocks with slots for gunwales are a good option if you don't have a luggage rack or roof racks.
- If you find an older fiberglass boat in need of repair, be sure you know what's involved. Boats with cored hulls (fiberglass "skins" over plywood, foam, or other core material) may have more damage than you care to fix.
- Our favorite camp boat was a Klepper folding kayak. Klepper construction is a wood rib-and-stringer system which snaps together and comes apart with no tools. Fabric and rubber shape the hull; air tubes provide flotation. Ours even had a sailing rig. Taken apart, it packed into four bags, easier to carry than a solid dinghy. We have many fond, forever memories connected with that boat.

bring a small boat; the hard part may be in choosing the right one.

If you're preparing for eventual canoe or sea kayak camping, the choice is made; you'll need an adequate size to accommodate the gear. However, smaller kayaks are extremely popular, just for the fun of them.

If you want a small rowboat for fishing, sightseeing, or simply drifting and dreaming, look for a suitable used boat that can be carried on top of the car. Check classifieds, flea markets and garage sales, bulletin boards at local marinas or lakeside campgrounds. You'll probably start with the boat only, later possibly adding a small outboard or trolling motor.

"Small" is probably somewhere between 10 and 14 feet long; look at an aluminum jonboat (somewhat rectangular in shape, and relatively stable), an inflatable (like the Cousteau team made so popular), or a fiberglass skiff, either flat-bottomed or tri-hull.

One company—PortaBote—manufactures a polypropylene boat that actually folds down to a flat 4 inches (see illustration, page 119).

You can probably rent a boat initially, but when you decide to buy one, find a knowledgeable friend to help you choose. Check the library for background information; learn your state's boating regulations, equipment requirements, and safety recommendations; then, get a carry rack for the car, tie the boat on, and find some water.

# CAMERA FUN

Photography is one of camping's most popular pastimes. Everyone brings some sort of camera, because photography can be enjoyed on so many levels.

## Family Photos

First are the snapshots—not just to record where you go, but more significantly, to show what you do together.

These days, most families have video cameras, and while videos do add a dimension to camping memories, they should not be the exclusive record. To take the kind of photos that make those memories, go for the candid, not the smiling lineup shots. Try to capture the feeling of the place by catching the feelings people have about the place. With the availability of "throwaway" cameras that come with film, children can take their own version of fun at camp. Give each child a roll of film and ask them to take pictures of what they think is best about camping. The results may not win prizes, but they will be revealing. Later, the pictures become part of each camper's diary or scrapbook—and you keep the dupes. (And yes, the throwaway film cases are recyclable now.)

As older children show the interest, challenge them to create a photo-record of each area you visit, telling their travel story in pictures rather than words. Challenge yourself to do the same. Digital cameras make such efforts fun. Because of their computer connection, they've revived interest in sharing family photos.

## Wildlife Photography

Wildlife photography is a specialty niche; the simple fact that you usually cannot get too close to your subject demands more sophisticated gear than a point-and-shoot.

You can practice at home with the backyard squirrels. Study their daily routine and plan the pic-

*Cameras help you create memories and art.*

tures you'd like to catch—but always be ready to abandon the plan if something unexpected happens. Once you're out of the yard and into the wild, you may find a similar situation of watching some resident wildlife. Always remember that the animals are *wild*; even small animals can get nasty if they feel threatened. Most wild animals sense a "safe" space; if you move into theirs, they're gone.

Assuming you manage to see an animal before it sees you, try to stalk it, for more natural pictures. You're probably downwind already, or you wouldn't have gotten into a position of seeing it first. Move slowly and quietly; the animal's eyes may not be keen, but its nose and ears are. Move a bit, then wait a bit. Crouch down when necessary to hide your silhouette. Make your first picture count; the first camera click, and your prey will be gone.

If you're a patient photographer, a boardwalk over marshland is a good place to plant a tripod and wait. (If you set up, they will come.) Sitting quietly at a spring, pond, or marsh is a great way to

see and photograph wildlife, especially at dawn and dusk.

Capturing wilderness images without the wildlife is much easier. You pick time and place,

*Tripod keeps camera steady and level on uneven surfaces.*

## Photo Fun

- If your camera is waterproof, you won't worry so much about getting caught in the rain. Nikonos is famous for underwater use, but many other companies make weather-resistant cameras.
- As Ansel Adams so beautifully demonstrated, nature is a willing subject for black-and-white photography, though to be able to explore it fully you need a home darkroom.
- Don't disrupt wildlife just for a picture. Leave nesting birds alone, and don't frighten deer. Don't attempt to feed any wild animals to bring them within camera range. If you're serious about stalking wildlife for candid pictures, wear earth tones or a real camouflage pattern so you, too, can blend with the surroundings.

# FAMILY FUN

What's a campfire without a songfest? The answer depends partly on where you are, but bring along the recorder or flute, harmonica or guitar, if there's room in the car. Bring the instruments, even if you don't have a campfire; music is a universal joy, even for the monotones among us.

To avoid a chorus of la-las and da-di-das, print out the words to some good sing-along songs. Maybe use your handy PC to print them in a large typeface so they'll be more readable by the campfire or lantern glow. Be prepared with extra copies: the circle of singers usually grows.

Camping is an ideal way to stay in touch with family. If you don't all live in the same city, visits are too often limited to a couple of holidays each year, with a possible vacation trip in between. But if you can meet halfway in a camping situation, you can see each other more weekends during the summer in the relaxed surroundings of the tent-away-from-home. Everyone shares camping chores, so nobody has to play hostess.

If well planned, an extended family reunion could practically fill the campground, and provide more than the usual four or five hours of a picnic to try to establish how you relate to who. Cousins have a chance to know more about each other than name, age, and last year's birthday present.

Friends also keep in touch this way. So many people move so often with job changes or company relocations, it's difficult to maintain long-distance friendships. But an annual vacation week in a different part of the country lets everyone see new places while they renew old relationships.

and carefully compose postcard pictures: reflections in a pond mirror, a hillside of autumn reds and russets, spring's explosion of greens.

Sunsets are beautiful to the beholder, but a photo of a sunset often needs a foreground silhouette to frame the event.

Plants and flowers are obliging subjects: They stay put for as long as it takes to decide which is the best composition, or which is their best side. They'll even wait for the light to be right. Take them in overview or close up. Try the wide-angle lens, if you have a choice of lenses, to include the backdrop of meadow or woods.

# *SPECIAL CAMPING*

## 17

Once the daily routine of camping life becomes second nature, you may find yourself wondering, "What's next?" Should you continue driving to farther destinations—there are still lots of places on your list—or should you consider a different way to get to those destinations, with all the attendant changes that would bring?

You could start a whole new phase of outdoor living, one where you won't have the option of going to a motel to avoid the rain, or ordering a pizza to replace a forgotten meal. Sometimes, you won't even be able to change your mind and go home—not without a lot of the kind of effort you may want to avoid. These non-choices are part of minimalist camping, where canoeists and kayakers paddle remote rivers, backpackers hike mountain trails, and bicyclists explore country byways. The rewards, however, can outweigh any downside, provided you're prepared—mentally, physically, and by having the right equipment.

## CANOE CAMPING

Canoe camping is the logical follow-up to car camping. The canoeist can take much of the same type of gear, especially if items were originally chosen with the idea of a someday canoe trip.

Canoeing may be the only access (short of bush plane) into some wilderness areas, and getting there is more than half the fun. Canoe speed lets you see, and canoe silence lets you enjoy, so much more of the natural surroundings.

The first requisite: Everybody knows how to swim. The second: Be sure a canoe trail matches your skill level.

## Learn to Canoe

Nobody learns how to paddle a canoe by reading about it. For the best start, find an outfitter and sign up for lessons. You'll meet other beginners, and may be able to organize a joint canoe trek with the outfitter as leader. As with any new skill, it's easier to learn the right habits than to break wrong ones.

Before you buy a canoe, do the rental route till you find a type you like. Look at aluminum, fiberglass, or lighter-weight composites. Rent different hull designs, so you can make an informed decision when the time comes to buy. For family camping, look for load-carrying ability and stability—probably a shallow-V hull. Parents and two children can all fit into one canoe when the kids are small; later, you may prefer to buy or rent a second canoe.

Study the paddles you rent, too. Blade width will affect how far you move with each stroke, and how tired you get in the process. Best recommendation: buy four paddles with your canoe; you'll need spares.

## Load the Canoe

It's most important to balance the load in the canoe. If it's bow-heavy, you won't be able to steer; if stern-heavy, the canoe will try to steer itself. "Tippy" says a lot about excess weight on one side. The ideal is to load the canoe so it sits perfectly level in the water, when it's full of gear and paddlers.

Check the load capacity (printed on a metal plate attached to the canoe, usually near the stern)

Keep weight centered
when loading canoe.

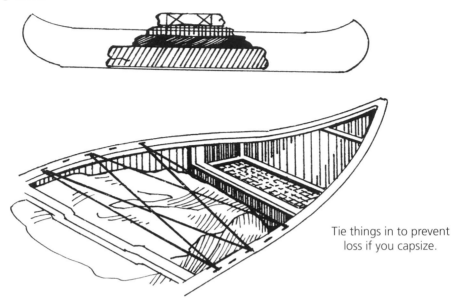

Tie things in to prevent
loss if you capsize.

for an idea of the amount of stuff you'll be able to carry (or not). Before loading, put all gear into waterproof bags, especially the tent, sleeping bags, packs, and duffels that would suffer from a soaking. Use a watertight dry box for important things like cameras, fire starters, and stoves.

Start loading, heaviest items on the bottom, centered side to side and more or less centered lengthwise (any adjustment here being to compensate for paddlers of unequal weight). Don't stack bags any higher than about 6 inches above the top of the canoe or it will be top-heavy.

Last items in are the people; climb in, and check to see that the canoe is level. Repack, if necessary, and when everything's in a satisfactory spot, tie it all securely in place.

## Accidental Unloading

If you've been using a canoe as the daytime fun boat on car camping trips, you may have already done a capsize drill. If not, take some lessons in canoe capsize from an outfitter or dealer. Let the children help with the "overturn" part (seldom do they have such an opportunity to do what they should *not* do). Once it's flipped, everybody hangs on and pushes the canoe to shore.

## Safety First

Of course, the children will wear *PFDs* (personal flotation devices) at all times on or near the water. For younger children, look for the type with a flotation collar and leg loops that keep the vest in place, preventing a ride-up. (Sad statistic: more boating fatalities involve anchored boats under 16 feet than larger boats.)

## Charts and Maps

In most places, your topographic maps will suffice for navigation, but some areas will be better covered by nautical charts or river maps. These will show water depths, as well as prominent land-

# Paddling Tips

- Board with the least amount of lateral weight shift; step slowly into the center of the canoe, transferring weight from dock or shore to canoe with steady motion, not a jump or jerk. Step out the same way.
- While the front seat position usually requires the strongest paddler, if a parent and one child are paddling the canoe, the child usually takes the front seat.
- When canoeing, you don't always have a choice of getting in out of the rain. Buy good-quality rainsuits for everybody.
- Study the water ahead for possible dangers; look well down-stream for a general sense of your route.
- An upstream V shows water flowing around a rock or wood snag.
- A downstream V means water flow is being pinched between rocks or shallow banks.
- A *pillow* of water indicates a rock or other obstruction. (The water swirls in a pillow shape as it flows over and around the obstruction.)
- At a bend, water is deepest on the side scoured by current flow.

- Check for *eddies* (backwaters) where you can safely stop.
- If you're new to the waters, stop well above any rapids and assess the situation on foot. If there's any question of safety, *portage* the gear (carry it overland around the rapid); then, if you're still up for it, try the rapids with an empty canoe. *Lining* the canoe (towing it from shore) is a compromise option. If you do make many portages, it's easier to tote a backpack than a duffel bag.

## Basic Canoe Strokes

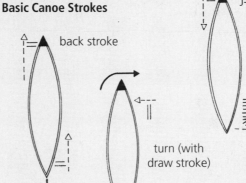

back stroke

turn (with draw stroke)

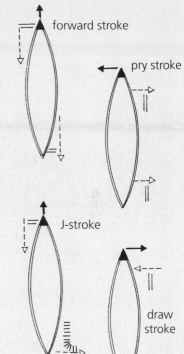

forward stroke

pry stroke

J-stroke

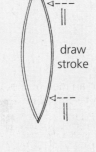

draw stroke

marks and shoreline features, so you can keep track of your position fairly easily. You may need to understand navigation markers and signs: buoys and channel markers that indicate safe navigation routes. (Get a booklet describing navigation rules from your state boat-registration agency.)

If your canoe route takes you across a lake or open bay, watch the weather carefully. While the water may be calm near shore, wind can quickly kick up waves in open water.

## Canoe Campsites

Along some canoe routes, you'll find complete campgrounds. Other areas may have designated sites at intervals along the route. Still others will be for strictly backcountry use, on a first-come, first-served basis: pick a spot and camp. If possible, camp well away from the water, just as you would at any other location.

Be sure to do your pre-camping research well; it is not fun to paddle three hours longer than

EUREKA

*Arriving at a campsite by water suggests a wilderness adventure, even if the site is not true backcountry.*

planned, and it is downright frightening to be paddling around a strange river after dark. Arrange your days with plenty of leeway. Give yourself ample time to set up camp and enjoy the scenery before nightfall. For longer-than-day trips, allow for bad-weather days.

## Canoe Repair

Be prepared for making temporary repairs in case of canoe damage. You can buy or put together a kit of "real" materials, or rely on Old Faithful: silver duct tape. Overlapping strips of everybody's favorite emergency stuff will patch the typical hole, and permanent repairs can be done later at home.

## People Repair

Take a more complete first-aid kit, with the how-to book more specifically directed to medical care in wilderness surroundings.

# BACKPACKING

For some backpackers, cross-country travel is the only way to go. The essence of backpacking is a real back-to-nature experience, and they are most protective of "their" wilderness. But not all backpackers are long-distance wanderers. Anyone can take a dayhike with a daypack, and many families do just that, walking into a backcountry site for the weekend. All it takes is willingness, preparation, and the right equipment.

Backpacking gear is not exactly back-to-basics; quite the opposite, it borders on state-of-the-art. Backpackers must carry everything they need: food, water (filter), clothing, cooking and sleeping gear. Size and weight are critical; priorities are measured and balanced in inches and ounces.

The backpack is a marvel of design. Besides the primary function of holding so much equipment, the pack must be carryable for hours, not just short trips. The typical backpacker carries 35 to 50 pounds. Gear must be packed to distribute weight evenly so it rides properly. *It* must fit the person's frame, not the other way around.

# BIKE CAMPING

Bicyclists find the real back roads the car traveler never sees, and in doing so, discover the people and places of America's real hometowns. Besides the fitness benefit, bicycling saves gas.

Bicycle campers take the same lightweight equipment as backpackers, but the weight is on their bike, not their back. Bike packs are called *panniers*, or *saddlebags;* some are mounted over the rear tire, some over the front. Bicycle campers may stay at campgrounds alongside car campers, and they have an option not usually available to

## Biking

Biking has a few advantages over backpacking: the weight of equipment is on the bike, not the back. Bikers don't have to carry much food; they can resupply daily. Bikers can stop biking whenever and wherever they choose. Remember: duct tape doesn't work on bicycles. Carry a repair kit. Take what you can to repair tires, brakes, and chain. (Bike shops can recommend tools and parts.)

canoeist or backpacker: they can stay at a motel if they get weary of the minimalist approach. Bicycle campers don't have to carry a lot of food—they can stop daily if they choose.

## Backpacking

There are three basic types of packs. External-frame packs have a visible, H-shaped frame with the pack attached. The load is carried higher on shoulders. Internal-frame packs are most popular now; the weight is carried lower, and there is less tendency for the pack to throw the hiker off balance, although you tilt forward more. Rucksacks, or daypacks, have no frame, and are usually used just for day trips.

You can buy a pack for your hiking dog, too!

### Backpacking Food

- Backpackers who plan a five- or six-month hike on a long trail like the Appalachian Trail sometimes have a friend ship food boxes to post offices along the way. Hikers exit the trail at regular intervals; they can shop in towns, but some prefer to use the specialized foods not usually stocked in local stores.
- Typical hiker's breakfast: gra-

nola bars, dried fruit eaten while walking. Lunch: bagels with cheese, salami, peanut butter. All filling items that travel well.
- A man may lose 30 pounds on a long hike. (Women usually don't lose as much weight.)
- From a weight and space perspective, the best food to take camping—especially backpacking—is dried food. Instead of buying commercially prepared and packaged meals, many backcountry campers dry their own.
- Fruits and vegetables, meats, cheese, even eggs can be home dried. An actual food dryer may be the most efficient means, but once food is appropriately cut, diced, or sliced, it can be dried in other ways, too. With all methods, timing will be "till dry."
- To sun-dry food, place all food on screens in direct sun. Screens should be raised about 8 inches off the ground so air circulates.

Cover with netting to discourage bugs or birds. Turn the food a few times during the day, and bring it inside at night.
- To oven-dry food, set oven at lowest temperature (probably 140°F); prop door open a bit; set food directly on racks, or on trays or cookie sheets.
- Some items (like herbs, green beans, pepper strips, apple slices) can be air-dried. Store all dried foods in the most airtight containers you own.

### Getting Fit

To prepare for a backcountry trek, walk, swim, jog, bike—whatever your usual keep-in-shape routine might be. Start slow and build up to strenuous days. (If you don't have a usual routine, rethink the advisability of the trip.)

While there are many fancy bikes to choose from, rental is again the first choice if you are just starting out. Find a bicycle shop, join a bicycling club, read a bicycling magazine.

# SPECIAL GEAR

Whether you're canoeing, backpacking, or bicycling, the most obvious place to start shrinking camp gear is the tent. You wouldn't—you couldn't—carry a big cabin tent. For the family, two smaller tents will be easier to manage.

Specialty camping is where you find a lot of interesting niche equipment. Tent designs are works of art, shaped like contemporary cocoons and boasting names like Starstream, Windfoil, and Lightyear. Backpack tents have curved hoops for poles, to create as much interior volume as they can from a tent that might weigh as little as 6 or 7 pounds.

You can find a small tent with two entries—front and back doors—so each person can come and go without an awkward and disruptive climb-over. A few designs have two vestibules, too, to keep everything out of the main tent except the campers.

A *bivy (bivouac) bag*, with a cover made of waterproof/breathable fabric, combines a sleeping bag with the shelter of a tent.

The design details of mummy sleeping bags can be truly appreciated in a mountain trek in the fall. Every ounce of down will do its best to hold body heat inside the hooded, cocoon shape.

Backpackers can choose from a wide assortment of single-burner stoves, many of which burn more than one kind of fuel.

ZZ Corp. makes the tiny Sierra cookstove that burns wood, charcoal, or solid fuel and is equipped with a battery-driven blower. Since it burns whatever you find, you don't have to carry fuel. For information, call 800-594-9046.

The BakePacker (and also the Outback Oven) transforms a standard-size cookpot into a miniature oven.

*Specialty gear for backpackers includes tiny stoves.*

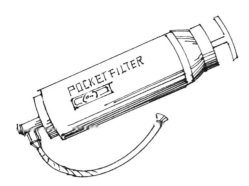

*A hand-operated water filter pump.*

Tiny candle lanterns light up tiny tents. And the once-simple flashlight now takes many new forms and a few new holders: headband, flex-neck, wrist-band.

Inspired by the popularity and longevity of Swiss Army knives, many companies now attach many tools onto a common handle for a versatile *multi-tool.*

If you like gadgets, look at a sport watch. One Casio model can tell you elevation, compass heading, temperature, barometric pressure, and, oh yes, time, in 12- or 24-hour readings.

Of course, there are no "backpacking" bottles for carrying a water supply; water is taken as needed from an available source, and purified with tablets (for short trips) or one of the hand-operated water filter pumps (see pages 110 and 146).

For backpacking, bike camping, and canoe routes with portages, a cooler is eliminated rather than replaced. Minimalist campers may carry dehydrated or freeze-dried foods, pre-packaged for breakfast, lunch, or dinner. These are expensive to buy, but you can easily dry and package your own favorite foods, an alternative many campers choose (see sidebar, page 127).

Others prefer to shop supermarket shelves, buying either prepared noodle or rice mixes, or putting together their own quick meals from pasta, rice, bouillon, sauces, and freeze-dried vegetables.

Even such quick meals will take longer to cook at some backpacking locations. With the decreased pressure of higher elevations, water boils at lower temperatures, so the food you're boiling will take a longer time to cook through. (For each 5,000-foot increase in elevation, boiling temperature drops about 10°F; at 5,000 feet, your three-minute egg will probably take six minutes to cook.)

## SPECIAL CLOTHES

Backpackers, expending the most energy, are the most likely specialty campers to pay attention to clothes layering: wearing *wickable* fabrics next to the skin to carry moisture away, so insulating layers can do their job. All backcountry campers need good rain gear, not having the immediate choice of getting in out of the rain.

For the heat and sun of a desert climate, cottons retain moisture, trapping it next to your skin to keep you cooler. Wide-brimmed hats are most important here to give you some shade.

For warmth at higher elevations and in cooler seasons, a down parka is most warm—and most expensive. Down is still the most efficient, most comfortable, most durable, lightest-weight insulation, but the same synthetic insulations used in sleeping bags are also found in outerwear, providing good alternatives.

## SPECIAL PLACES

UVB rays affect you more at high altitudes, so pay attention to protecting any exposed skin, like nose and ears. Also, you need good protection for your eyes, especially if glare from snow adds another factor.

**Mountains.** The most common complaint connected to higher elevations is that of altitude sickness. With a noticeable change in elevation, most people need some time for their bodies to adjust to less oxygen. A change of 5,000 or 6,000 feet would be noticeable, and may produce vague, flu-like symptoms: headache, fatigue, mild nausea, insomnia. There is no particular treatment or preventive; only time will help. Most people don't notice any effects from altitude till they are above 10,000 feet. Backpackers (through-hikers) plan for one- or two-day layovers at intervals, to allow their bodies to adjust.

**Wetlands.** Wetlands, by definition, won't have a lot of good (dry) campsites. In Florida's Everglades National Park, managers have come up with one solution for canoe-in campers: A few platforms have been built at the edge of mangrove islands.

*When setting up on a chickee platform, make "stakes" from metal rod; slide stakes between planks, turn bottom loop under and perpendicular to planks.*

You park your canoe, and set up camp on the platform (a *chickee*), which would be delightful were it not for the portable toilet housing at the end of the platform. This is one example of a place where a freestanding tent is necessary.

**Deserts.** People either love the starkness of a desert landscape, or they find it lonely and sad. For the stark-lovers, camping considerations include a tent site well away from any low-lying sand gullies. When choosing a desert campsite, keep to the highest ground, and find or make some shade.

If you must set up a tent on a rocky surface (whether desert plateau or rocky shoreline), place a heavy log alongside the tent and tie the tent to the log. Then weigh the log down with rocks. (If you can't find a log, use more rocks.)

**Beaches.** When camping on a coastal beach, the ideal campsite (from the viewpoint of prevent-

*Campsites for backpackers offer nothing but nature, which is either good or bad depending on the eye of the beholder.*

EUREKA

*The plus side for backpackers is that they go to places the rest of us see only through their photographs.*

ing erosion) is between the highest winter storm tide level, and the current high-tide level, where there's the least amount of vegetated surface to bother. This is not always easy to judge. (For more information on low-impact camping on the coast as well as in other areas, contact Leave No Trace, Inc. at 800-332-4100 or www.lnt.org.)

## Low-Impact Fires and Camping

If you ever camp in a truly pristine or un-impacted place, keep it that way. If you use a fire, make it a *mound fire,* to separate the fire's heat from the earth. With a firepan, it's easy: put the pan on a mound of rocks, gravel, or sand. Without the pan, build the mound of unburnable rock or "mineral soil" (dirt with no organic material) to form a buffer

between heat and earth. It takes very little effort for a real return: no charred, sterilized soil.

Keep the fire small and use only dead wood already on the ground—don't cut any tree limbs for fuel. Never leave a fire unattended, and always, always make sure you've doused the fire completely before leaving the campsite.

Many backpackers are very vocal in expressing their dislike for open fires: "They're dirty, smoky; burn wood unnecessarily; not good for heat: you burn one side and freeze the other; worst, you're killing that part of the Earth." Another view: "Stoves and fuel are products of extractive and environmentally degrading industry. When and when not to burn is a matter of wood availability, human use, environmental fragility, use of firepans, taking care with fire scars, and so on."

Practice low-impact camping in other ways.

When hiking, walk on the marked trail to prevent erosion and to keep surrounding vegetation and soils from being trampled. This is especially important in desert and alpine areas. When you take a break, rest on a durable surface like a rock slab. If you have a snack, be sure to pack out the wrapper and any leftovers; keep a zip-top bag in an outside pocket of your backback for easy access.

Don't mark your route with string or rocks. Instead, learn how to use a compass and topo map to keep track or your position.

If you've applied bug repellent or sunscreen, don't wash your hands or face in a lake or stream.

These products may be toxic to aquatic creatures. If you want to take a dip, first carry a jug of water away from the lake or stream and use it to rinse off.

Remember that it's illegal to collect feathers, antlers, rocks, bones, and plants on many public lands without a permit.

# WORDS OF CAUTION

All the specialized forms of camping require a buildup of strength and stamina, and unless everyone in the family is willing to put in the time, it will be wasted effort for those who do. But if everyone is agreeable, it opens yet another door, a back door to real backcountry camping.

# CAMP CLEANUP

## 18

Too soon, it seems, it's time to un-camp. Without the anticipation of fun, packing up to leave is everybody's least favorite aspect of camping.

Clearing up your site at a commercial campground is easy, if unexciting: take the trash to the recycling bins or the dumpster; sift the ashes one more time, wipe off the picnic table, and you're done. The wilderness camper, however, still has at least one more outdoor challenge to meet—to leave no trace. That means removing every trace of every item that you brought in, right down to the tiniest food wrapper, twist tie, and charcoal briquette.

## SORT THE TRASH

Regardless of where you camped, you've probably been separating trash as you accumulated it, either to deposit in the campground's assorted bins, or to pack out to the nearest disposal place.

Packing out the trash is really not much of a chore. You brought in a bunch of full containers—canned food, bottles, cans, or "boxes" of juices and soft drinks—so you can easily take out the same number of containers. "Easily," because they are now minus the weight of their contents.

Sort cans and bottles just as you normally do. While you are probably familiar with the categories of recyclables for your home trash disposal service, you should check regualtions in the area where you are camping. You will then be sure you are separating trash sensibly, and you will also learn the location of the nearest recycling bins or trash disposal containers.

If you crush all the aluminum cans, you'll have a smaller bag to carry to that recycler. While an official, handled can crusher does the neatest crushing to pancake flatness, two hands can do a respectable job of first denting, then folding an aluminum can, reducing its volume considerably. Stomping also has a flattening effect.

Any non-edible or no-longer-edible food leftovers should be thrown away, not buried. If you put food into the ground, some animal will just dig it right back up, and it probably won't refill the hole.

You've no doubt been feeding the campfire with any burnables you used: paper plates, paper towels, paper cups, and of course the strips of newspaper used for fire-starting. Check the fire pit now, and remove the remains of anything that did not go straight to ash, including (but not limited to) blobs of melted plastic, sparkly bits of foil,

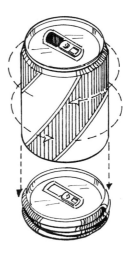

Twist and push sides in to dent.

Step on it.

the can opener that mysteriously disappeared on day one.

# STRIKE THE CAMP

If all clothes are headed for the laundry, line your duffel with a big plastic garbage bag before packing. Shake out each item of clothing before you pack it so you don't accidentally transplant some unsuspecting woodland bug who won't know how to live in a house.

For the same reason, shake out sleeping bags and mats, then roll them (or stuff them) neatly so they pack in the smallest space. Tie them closed if they don't have a personal stuff sack for containment.

Brush off the tent and other tarps, to remove the bits of twigs, leaves, and spider web. Wipe off the worst of any stains or spots with a damp cloth. Take the tent apart, packing poles and stakes in their bags, separate from the tent itself. Coil up all guylines and keep them in a bag to prevent premature unwinding.

If groundcloths are damp, shake them and hang them out for awhile as you finish other chores.

Pack all the cooking gear and other small items in their pre-assigned storage boxes or cooler. Any pots and pans used over a cook fire should be stored in bags to reduce the spreading of soot. Give the stove and lantern a quick wipe before closing them into their traveling locations; you don't want to give soot an opportunity to rub off on anything.

The cooler will probably have food or drinks in it that you want to keep handy for a home-bound snack stop. Remove most of the water to eliminate the slosh and clang of swimming containers.

If you planned well, packing up car or canoe will be a repeat of the starting exercise. The more often you go through the routine, the more of a habit the arrangement will become. When everything's packed, turn your attention back to the campsite, and think "natural."

# RESTORE THE SITE

The guidelines of the Leave No Trace association are all aimed at encouraging campers to leave the wilderness as they found it—or better. With that in mind, the whole family should get involved in restoring the campsite.

If you moved any rocks or logs to make seats, table supports, or cooking counters, put them back where you found them. (Who's in charge of the site map???)

Where vegetation is flattened or matted from

## Packing Up

- At campgrounds with a bathhouse, count shower kits and accessories, towels and facecloths, and watches.
- Also check the dryer at the self-service laundry, for the beach towels.
- Pack out leftover food items; they won't degrade for a long time, and wildlife will dig them up.
- Don't forget to cut apart six-pack rings. Even though the plastic is degradable, it doesn't happen quickly; birds, animals, fish, and turtles can still get caught in them in the interim if any plastic manages to evade the trash.

- Don't throw a whole bucketful of water on a fire in one big splash, or you'll cause a big cloud of steam dripping with ash. Pour a small, steady stream instead.
- Don't just pour water over charcoal briquettes; soak the coals in water.
- Some campers think it's okay to bury leftover coals from the fire pit, after they've been thoroughly doused with water. But, Smokey says no: "They can smolder and break out."
- Nine out of 10 forest fires are caused by people.
- If you ever see a curl of smoke

rising where none should be, report it to the closest responsible person: park employee, town police, or fire department.
- In former camping days, considerate campers left a small stack of firewood so the next campers would have a start on their supply. Nowadays, extra firewood may not be available.
- Anywhere, leave a campsite in better condition than it was when you arrived. In the wilderness, try to leave it so it looks truly untouched.

weight or from walking, brush it back up with a branch, to give it a head start on renewal. If you have firewood left, scatter it around for someone to "find."

Re-cover the patch of earth you so carefully cleared for the tent floor; replace the pinecones, pebbles, branches and twigs. Exact positioning is less important than an overall random look

If your campfire's still glowing, douse it with water. Stir the ashes a bit, add more water, and stir again. Continue this procedure till you can touch the ground (and any rocks around the fire pit) and feel no heat. (If you don't have a lot of water, use dirt; keep mixing it with the embers and ash till everything is cool.) Even if the fire was put out last night, give it one more splash, one more stir. Redundancy is good where fire is concerned.

If your wilderness camp included a wilderness bathroom, refill all holes and replace whatever natural cover was there before you dug.

Take another look around; don't leave any bits of twine around a tree, any broken stakes in the ground. And if your pet has been camping with you, don't leave any obvious evidence of its presence.

Now—finally—comes a fun part. When all the camping gear is packed, and the movable stuff has been replaced, give each child a fallen tree branch (preferably one with a lot of little branches still attached) and send them around the campsite to sweep away all signs of your temporary habitation. These are the heroes, foiling the bad guys by fooling the tracker. When they're happy with their efforts, scatter the branches, take one more picture, and start thinking about next time.

# APRÈS CAMP

# *READY*

## 19

For a summer vacation schedule, the ideal situation would be to unload the car after camping and put everything directly into the dedicated storage area where it would be ready and waiting for the next departure.

Reality involves an extra unpacking and repacking to allow for more thorough cleaning, necessary repairs, and neater storage. Set up a routine to follow, and it won't seem much of a chore.

## TENTS AND TARPS

If you weren't able to clean and dry the tent at camp before packing up, set it up in the yard. If it needs cleaning, hose it down or use a sponge to get rid of mud and leaves, taking special care to remove spots from bird droppings or tree drippings. Use warm water and a mild soap, like Ivory flakes, Dr. Bronner's soap, or the liquid hand soap you buy in pump bottles. Don't use detergents or bleach; they may damage the fabric or waterproof coating. (When in doubt, refer to the care label of your tent.)

It is most important that the tent be completely dry before packing, so mildew doesn't have a chance. If it's raining when you come home, set up the tent in the basement or garage.

Some campers keep the tent in its carry bags; others accordion-fold it loosely and hang it over a padded hanger, or lay it on a shelf.

Look for any places where the fabric is starting to get thin from chafing, and reinforce it before it becomes a hole. Ripstop tape (an adhesive-backed reinforced fabric) can help, but patching with tent fabric will be most permanent. See your handy tent repair kit.

If a repair kit was not part of your original tent purchase, buy one or put one together so that whenever you need something, it's handy. Include some tent fabric, screening, sewing items, patching tape, and fabric glue.

You'll also need seam sealer, a water-repellent coating to spray or brush on. Tent seams need to be sealed from time to time. Generally, resealing once a season is sufficient, but check seams occasionally. If you start seeing too many pinpoints of light, it might be time.

Spray lubricants might help a stubborn zipper, but they can also stain the fabric. When zippers don't work smoothly, the first step is to wash with warm, soapy water; it may be an attack of killer grit. Also try rubbing them with trusty old bar soap or a wax candle.

If the zipper pull is bent, you can get a replacement at an outdoor supply store or a fabric shop.

Watch pole ends for corrosion or scratches. Sand them with a fine wet-or-dry paper and spray with silicone lubricant. Replace bent poles before the weak leg causes others to buckle.

When the shock cord in your poles starts to lose its spring, buy a replacement kit and restring the poles. Put a leader on the cord so it threads through without bunching.

If a tent peg seems to bend too readily, consider replacing them all with stronger stakes, before it becomes necessary.

Not surprisingly, major repairs (on tents, sleeping bags, packs) are done at shops that specialize in outdoor gear. Check your retailer or the manufacturer for a recommendation. (When stitching starts to go in a few places, it probably means *all* the thread is getting weak. If the tent fabric's still

# Care And Repair

## Tents

To apply seam sealer to your tent. Set up the tent outside so it's warm, but don't apply sealer in direct sun. Clean the seams with rubbing alcohol. If the tent's instructions don't specify, apply the sealer to the inside seams of the tent floor (or the tub seams, where the floor attaches). Also seal all rain fly seams. (Some campers think all seams—inside and outside—should be sealed.) Seam sealer can also plug the tiny voids on packs and rainwear.

After using sealer, don't fold the tent (or jacket or pack) until the sealant is well set.

Screening can be patched with self-adhesive transparent Mylar, or with patch kits to be sewn in place.

If the rain fly needs to be replaced, choose a light color to reflect sun, deflect heat.

## Special Materials

- To keep down from lumping or matting as it dries, put a few tennis balls in the dryer. (Clean tennis *shoes* have also been suggested: lightweight sneakers.)
- Buy a special soap recommended for washing down.
- It's most important to remove all soap residue from down. You may have to send it through the washer a second time for water-only rinsing.

- If in doubt about proper care, call the manufacturer.
- Vinyl, rubber, and different types of plastic can be tricky to repair; what fixes one may melt another (and sometimes, "melting" is desirable). Keep the material-identification labels from products you buy; when they need repair, you'll know what to look for. If you don't find the right adhesive for your application, call the manufacturer and ask for a recommendation.
- Outdoor Goop (a real product) works to seal and glue a lot of different materials—even to glue the sole back on a sandal.

## Miscellaneous

- Propane stoves need little maintenance; just keep them clean and check for leaks. (Having fewer parts to replace is one of the propane stove's advantages over liquid fuel.)
- As one more way to fight a lingering odor in a cooler, wipe the interior with a cloth saturated with vanilla extract, then leave the cloth in the cooler overnight. (Store cooler in a cool, dry place; avoid hot attics or car trunks.)
- Left alone, mildew will rot the

material it has adopted as home. Wash the item; treat with mild solution of chlorine bleach or lemon juice; leave out in sunshine.
- Goop hand cleaner (no relation to the adhesives) is a good stain remover for washable fabrics. Spread it over spots before washing.
- Fiberglass boats and canoes are fairly easy to fix with a patch of fiberglass cloth or mat coated with some epoxy resin.
- Small dings on aluminum boats or canoes can be fixed with Liquid Aluminum, a putty that dries to a sandable hardness. Major dents can be reshaped by an automobile body shop.
- If you store sleeping bags in a closet, they should be draped over cushioned hangers or thick dowels set up specifically for the bags.
- Label the sleeping bag hangers by owner if two or more of the sleeping bags are the same color.
- Hang the tent, too, over a cushioned hanger to avoid creases.
- Boxes can all be stacked in a geometric arrangement, just like the closet organizer ads.
- Don't consider the attic for winter storage unless it's well insulated. Cold can make rubber and plastic brittle.

good, have it resewn before the great unravel.) A lot of the better gear is covered by an extended warranty, and in many cases will be repaired or replaced by the manufacturer.

# SLEEPING BAGS

After each use, air the bags inside out in sunshine for a few hours. (Or toss them into the dryer, one by one.)

When sleeping bags need to be washed, it's easiest to take a trip to the nearest self-service laundry. Not only do the bags wash better in the large, front-loading machines (a bag could wrap around the agitator of a top loader and cause the machine to dance a merengue), but you can use as many machines as you need to wash all the bags at once, one bag per machine. Here's where you'll appreciate synthetic insulation: it dries a lot faster than down.

After washing, spray the sleeping bag shell with a water-repellent coating; it will stay clean longer.

If you wear clothes to bed, or use a sheet liner, the *inside* of the bag will stay cleaner longer.

Down bags can be washed—carefully—in a large washer with mild soap on a gentle cycle (check label instructions). Hand washing is also suggested, but to call that tedious is an understatement. Dry the bag at a low-heat setting, for as long as it takes. Sometimes, dry cleaning is an option, but be sure the shop has experience with down.

Don't store a down bag in its stuff sack (compressing it into a tiny package is desirable only while you're camping). Roll or fold the bag loosely, and keep it in a laundry bag or a big pillow sham.

# MATTRESS PADS

## Air Mattresses

When rubberized canvas air mattresses need to be cleaned, sponge-wash the canvas with mild soap and warm water; then rinse with a hose and leave the mattresses outside to dry thoroughly. Roll them up loosely and store side by side (not stacked) on a cool shelf.

If your vinyl inflatable mattress springs a leak, buy an appropriate sealer to plug the pin hole. Manufacturers usually have repair products and kits.

## Self-inflating Pads

If you use the self-inflating foam mattress pads, leave them inflated when stored. They take more room in the closet, but the foam will last longer if it's not in a constant state of crush. Also, any moisture that may be inside will be able to escape.

Use self-adhesive tape to put a temporary patch on a rip in the cover of your mattress pad. If some of the foam has been gouged, push a small piece of sponge into the hole to level out the pad before attaching the fabric patch.

# STOVES

The orifice on a liquid-fuel stove burner gets clogged after a while and needs to be cleaned out with the tiny wire device in your maintenance kit. (Kerosene is a quicker clogger.)

Some liquid-fuel stoves are made to be self-cleaning. If this doesn't seem to be working, and it's possible to take the burner apart, soak the jet in some of the fuel the stove burns. When all cleaning attempts fail, replace the burner.

The pressure pumping handle will need a new O-ring or gasket sometime.

# LANTERN

Treat liquid-gas lantern burners the same as stove burners. Also, burn out the fuel rather than let it sit for any length of time. If you didn't buy a lantern case, leave the light in its "wastebasket" travel holder. Check your supply of spare mantles and add to the "buy" list when needed.

# COOLER

Empty the cooler and wash it as soon as you get home. Don't wait till morning, because you'll forget and by the time you're ready for the next trip you'll be growing a good crop of mildew and mold.

Hose down the outside to get rid of general camp dirt quickly; then wash the cooler inside and out with soap and warm water. If the cooler hangs onto a faint odor of onions, pickles, or whatever else leaked, wash it again with baking soda and water, or a mild solution of chlorine bleach and water. Wipe it partially dry, then prop open the lid so it can air-dry completely. Don't forget to clean the drain plug; it usually needs some extra attention to get rid of food or mold clogs.

Don't use abrasive kitchen cleansers on a cooler, especially on interior surfaces. The more you scrub, the more you'll have to scrub next time, because dirt will catch in all the tiny scratches made by the cleanser.

Wash out the assortment of drink containers: pitchers, thermos bottles, insulated pour-spout jugs. Start with hot water and soap. If you still detect orange juice or fruit punch, try the baking soda or bleach rinse. Sometimes, you may have to let them soak overnight with the deodorizing solution.

Covered plastic containers are great for cooler storage, but they, too, absorb the odor of the foods they're storing. Clean any plastic jars or boxes by rinsing with a bit of lemon juice (bottled okay) followed by a plain-water rinse.

# PORTABLE POT

Toilet cleaning must be Earth's most hated chore, and calling it portable doesn't change the situation one bit. It's too nasty even to use as punishment (as in, "Do this or you'll have to clean the pot").

Most likely, you took advantage of the campground's dump station to empty the holding tank and rinse it a few times with fresh water. Now, use the spray nozzle on the garden hose to do a pressure wash of all exposed surfaces. Then fill the holding tank with some baking soda (or bleach)

and water, and soak for a few hours. Then rinse, and rinse again.

Don't use abrasive cleansers on this smooth plastic surface, either.

# BACKYARD BOATYARD

Don't store your new canoe (or your old boat) upright outdoors, unless you want to start a mosquito farm. Flip it upside down, and prop it on some wood or cement blocks. Tie it down, if it's in a place open to a lot of wind.

Some campers hang the canoe from the ceiling in the garage. Upright's okay indoors; use S-hooks and pulleys at each end.

# CAMP CORNER

It's acceptable to store the canoe somewhere else, but the rest of the camping gear should be in one place. With closet space usually at a premium, that's not always possible, but it will make camping life so much easier if you can set aside a closet, or a corner of the basement or garage. It would be difficult to forget a box if it was the only item left in the camp corner. Not impossible, but difficult.

A good source of information for all your equipment repair needs is *The Essential Outdoor Gear Manual: Equipment Care, Repair, and Selection*, 2nd edition, by Annie Getchell and Dave Getchell Jr. (Ragged Mountain Press, 2000).

# CHECKLIST

An equipment list that covers all camping categories is necessarily overkill. Your own list must be based on your variables: carrying capacity, cooking methods, lighting options, individual priorities.

The following master list, broken down into categories, should give you a good start with your own list. Once you've settled on those items applicable to your kind of camping and cooking, you can either make copies of the list (one for each trip) or put it on ledger paper so you'll have a row of vertical check-off columns (one for each trip).

Tack the master list onto a bulletin board and hang it in the camping corner. With the "Campers' Needs" list, you'll want to make a copy for each person, so everyone can do their own packing and checking.

1. Camp Setup
2. Food Preparation and Storage
3. Campers' Needs
4. Your Choice
5. Canoe/Kayak/Other Boat
6. Car
7. Dog

## Camp Setup

__ Tent
__ Awning
　__ Poles
　__ Stakes and spares
　__ Guylines and 100 feet of extra ⅛-inch nylon line
__ Groundcloth
__ Sleeping bags
　__ Sleeping bag liners
__ Sleep pads or air mattresses
　__ Foot pump (for inflating air mattresses)
__ Pillows
__ Blankets
__ 1 or 2 tarps
__ Repair kit
　__ Ripstop tape
　__ Duct tape
　__ Length of pipe (for tent pole sleeve)
　__ Snap fastener kit or grommet kit
　__ Small sewing kit with safety pins
　__ Scissors
__ Folding chairs
__ Lantern
　__ Extra mantles
　__ Fuel (liquid gas or propane cylinder)
　__ Gas lighter, matches
__ Battery-operated lamp
　__ Extra batteries and bulb
__ Flashlight(s)
__ Extra batteries and bulb(s)
__ Candles
__ Candle holders
__ Electric cord
__ Electric light
__ Electric heater (*above three items if electricity available*)
__ Radio (weather)
　__ Batteries
__ Water hose
__ Water bottles (for ferrying)
__ Water filter or tablets
__ Mosquito coils
__ Dishwashing
　__ Portable sink (*or dish pan/wash bowl/rinse bottle*)

- __ Bucket
- __ Dish soap
- __ Kitchen cleanser
- __ Scrubbing pads
- __ Dishcloth or sponge
- __ Dish towel
- __ Clothesline
  - __ Clothespins
- __ Portable toilet
  - __ Holding tank treatment
- __ Shovel (fire, latrine)
- __ Wood saw or hatchet (firewood)
- __ Work gloves
- __ Pocket knife/multitool
- __ Utility straps
- __ Short shock (bungee) cords
- __ Block and tackle (if desired, for hanging food bag)

## Food Preparation and Storage

- __ Camp stove and fuel
  - __ Repair kit
- __ Firepan
- __ Firewood
- __ Propane or charcoal grill and fuel
- __ Fire-starting helps: newspaper, kindling, paraffin fire starters, gas lighter, matches
- __ Grill platform
- __ Pots
  - __ 1 large frying pan
  - __ 1 small frying pan
  - __ 2 or 3 saucepans, preferably with lids (or cook set of nesting pots and pans)
  - __ Disposable foil baking pans
- __ Non-stick cooking spray
- __ Coffee funnel and filters
- __ Cooking utensils
  - __ Aluminum foil
  - __ Flame tamer
  - __ Pliers or pot lifter
  - __ Oven mitts
  - __ Spatula
  - __ Tongs

- __ Skewers
- __ Large stirring spoon
- __ Ladle
- __ 2 sharp knives
- __ Mechanical can opener
- __ Bottle opener
- __ Potato peeler
- __ Cheese grater
- __ Cutting board
- __ Fish filleting board and knife
- __ Dining
  - __ Dinner plates
  - __ Soup/salad/cereal bowls
  - __ Mugs
  - __ Plastic glasses
  - __ Silverware
  - __ Paper-plate holders
  - __ Paper plates
  - __ Paper towels (use as napkins, too)
  - __ Tablecloth
- __ Miscellaneous
  - __ Plastic food bags
  - __ Zip-top bags
  - __ Garbage bags
  - __ Twist ties
- __ Optional
  - __ Bean pot tripod
  - __ "Spit" cooking setup
  - __ Wood chips for smoke flavor
  - __ Long griddle for camp stove
  - __ Measuring cup
  - __ Mixing bowl
  - __ Dutch oven
  - __ Reflector oven
  - __ Hanging bean pot
  - __ Grilled-sandwich maker/pie iron
  - __ Broiler basket
  - __ Popcorn popper
  - __ Hot dog fork
  - __ Icepick
  - __ Toothpicks
  - __ Corkscrew
  - __ Tablecloth clamps

- __ Foam-rubber can holders
- __ Lap trays
- __ Food "tent" (tabletop)
- __ Cooler
  - __ Small jars for ketchup, mayo, mustard, relish, jams
  - __ Ice supplements (home-frozen block ice, or blue coolant freezer packs)
  - __ Covered plastic containers for leftovers
  - __ Egg holder
  - __ Juice mixer/pitcher
- __ Don't forgets
  - __ Salt and pepper
  - __ Spice kit (include dehydrated vegetable flakes)
  - __ Salad oil
  - __ Coffee
  - __ Tea
  - __ Instant milk
  - __ Sugar
  - __ Marshmallows
- __ Food list and menus, your choice (for some suggestions and thoughts about camp cooking, see "Cookout Foods," beginning on page 152).

## Campers' Needs

- __ Duffel and pack
  - __ Long pants
  - __ Shorts
  - __ T-shirts
  - __ Flannel shirt and/or sweatshirt
  - __ Shoes/hiking boots
  - __ Spare walking shoes
  - __ Sneakers/moccasins
  - __ Socks
  - __ Underwear
  - __ Belt
  - __ Heavy sweatshirt and/or sweater
  - __ Windbreaker
  - __ Hat (wool and/or sun-shade)
  - __ Gloves
  - __ Sunglasses
  - __ Rainwear
  - __ Swimsuit
- __ Shower kit
  - __ Soap
  - __ Shampoo
  - __ Comb
  - __ Toothbrush/toothpaste
  - __ Dental floss
  - __ Razor

- __ Mirror
- __ Beach towel (optional)
- __ Bath towel
- __ Facecloth
- __ Facial tissues
- __ Toilet tissue
- __ Moist towelettes
- __ First aid/health
  - __ Alcohol swabs
  - __ Cotton swabs
  - __ Band-Aids
  - __ Moleskin
  - __ Gauze
  - __ Adhesive tape
  - __ Elastic bandage
  - __ Disinfectants (alcohol or hydrogen peroxide)
  - __ First aid cream
  - __ Eye patch
  - __ Tweezers
  - __ Clove (oil or powder)
  - __ Bug repellent
  - __ Bug bite treatment
  - __ Sunscreen
  - __ Sunburn treatment
  - __ Calamine lotion
  - __ Aspirin or acetaminophen
  - __ Ibuprofen (anti-inflammatory)
  - __ Antihistamine
  - __ Antacid
  - __ Anti-diarrheal
  - __ Snakebite kit
  - __ Personal medications

## Your Choice

- __ Bicycles
- __ Camera(s) and manual(s)
  - __ Film
- __ Video camera and manual
  - __ Blank tapes
- __ Binoculars
- __ Compass
- __ Topographic maps, nautical/river charts
- __ Sport watch with alarm
- __ Canteen/water bottles
- __ Daypacks/rucksacks
- __ Reference books
  - __ Birds, animals, plants, stars
- __ Writing notebook
- __ Musical instruments
- __ Games and puzzles

__ Ball or Frisbee
__ Fishing gear
__ Books for reading

## Canoe/Kayak/Other Boat

__ Roof racks (*or* foam blocks) and tie-down straps/
    ropes (for cartopping)
__ Paddles/oars
__ PFDs
__ Charts/maps
__ Compass
__ Waterproof bags
__ Flashlight
__ Line for gear tie-in and lining canoe
__ Repair kit
__ Outboard motor
   __ Gas can
__ Anchor
   __ Anchor line
__ Bailer
__ Sponge
__ Whistle

## Car

__ Wood blocks (wedges to block tires)
__ Spare tire and changing equipment
__ Jumper cables
__ Flares
__ Small tool kit
__ Spare engine belt
__ Spare hoses, fuses
__ Duct tape
__ Silver reflective tape
__ Engine oil
__ Compass
__ Road maps/atlases
__ Guidebooks
__ Travel games
__ Music/audiotapes
__ Picnic blanket
__ Moist towelettes
__ Whisk broom/dust pan
__ Small trash bags

## Dog

__ Dishes
__ Food

__ Harness/leash
__ Identification/health certificate
__ Brush
__ Pooper Scooper
__ Basket/pillow
__ Toy
__ Doggy pack

# CAMPING EQUIPMENT SOURCES

The following list of manufacturers and catalogs is just a sampling of what's out there. Find a camping/outdoor magazine, and check display and classified ads for more manufacturers and dealers.

## Manufacturers, Catalogs, Dealers

### General

Avid Outdoor
14760 Santa Fe Trail Drive
Lenexa, KS 66215
800-315-2267

Campmor, Inc.
29 Parkway
Upper Saddle River, NJ 07458
800-226-7667
www.campmor.com

Coleman
P.O. Box 2931
Dept. 586
Wichita, KS 67201-2931
800-835-3278
www.coleman.com

Don Gleason's Campers' Supply
P.O. Box 87
Northampton, MA 01061-0087
413-584-4895
www.gleasoncamping.com

REI (Recreational Equipment, Inc.)
P.O. Box 1700
Sumner, WA 98352
800-426-4840
www.rei.com

Sierra Designs
1255 Powell Street
Emeryville, CA 94608
800-736-8551
www.sierradesigns.com

**Tents**
Eureka!
625 Conklin Road
Binghamton, NY 13903
800-572-8822
www.eurekatent.com

Kelty
6235 Lookout Road
Boulder, CO 80301
800-423-2320
www.kelty.com

MSR
3800 1st Avenue S.
Seattle, WA 98134
800-550-8368
www.msrcorp.com

The North Face, Inc.
2013 Farallon Drive
San Leandro, CA 94577
800-447-2333
www.thenorthface.com

**Sleeping Bags**
Excel Outdoors
300 American Boulevard
Haleyville, AL 35565
800-221-7452

Gander Mountain
4567 W. 80th Street
Minneapolis, MN 55437
952-830-8700
www.gandermountain.com

Slumberjack
1224 Fernridge Parkway
St. Louis, MO 63141
800-233-6283
www.slumberjack.com

**Sleep Pads/Mattresses/Chairs**
Cascade Designs, Inc. (Therm-a-Rest)
4000 First Avenue S.
Seattle, WA 98134
800-531-9531
www.cascadedesigns.com

Crazy Creek Products
P.O. Box 1050
1401 South Broadway
Red Lodge, MT 59068
800-331-0304
www.crazycreek.com

Stearns Outdoors
P.O. Box 1498
St. Cloud, MN 56302
800-697-5801
www.stearnsinc.com

**Water Purification**
Exstream Water Technologies (Katadyn water filter)
1035 W. Bruce Street
Milwaukee, WI 53204
414-389-9868
www.katadyn.ch

PUR Products (water filter)
9300 N. 75th Avenue
Minneapolis, MN 55428
800-845-7873
www.purwater.com

WPC Brands (Potable Aqua tablets)
1 Repel Road
Jackson, WI 53037
800-558-6614
www.wpcbrands.com

**Navigation/Maps**
Brunton (compasses)
620 East Monroe Avenue
Riverton, WY 82501
800-443-4871
www.brunton.com

DeLorme Mapping Co.
P.O. Box 298

Yarmouth, ME 04096
207-846-7000
www.delorme.com

Garmin International (GPS)
1200 East 151st Street
Olathe, KS 66062
913-397-8200
www.garmin.com

Silva Compasses
625 Conklin Road
Binghamton, NY 13902
607-779-2200
www.jwa.com

Trails Illustrated (topographic maps)
P.O. Box 4357
Evergreen, CO 80437-4357
800-962-1643
www.trailsillustrated.com

U.S. Geological Survey Information Services
(topographic maps)
P.O. Box 25287
Denver, CO 80225
888-ASK-USGS (888-275-8747)
http://ask.usgs.gov/

### Stoves

Coleman
P.O. Box 2931
Dept. 586
Wichita, KS 67201-2931
800-835-3278
www.coleman.com

Wooska (Pyramid stoves)
P.O. Box 2397
Redmond, WA 98073
888-343-9100; 425-861-9522
www.wooska.com

ZZ Manufacturing, Inc.
P.O. Box 1798
Glendora, CA 91740
800-594-9046
www.zzstove.com

### Canoes and Kayaks

Klepper U.S.A.
18011 Sky Park Circle, Suite F
Irvine, CA 92614
800-500-2404
www.klepper.com

Mad River Canoe
P.O. Box 4339
Archdale, NC 27263
800-311-7245
www.madrivercanoe.com

Old Town Canoe Company
P.O. Box 548
Old Town, ME 04468
800-595-4400; 207-827-5514
www.oldtowncanoe.com

We-no-nah Canoe, Inc.
P.O. Box 247
Winona, MN 55987
507-454-5430
www.wenonah.com

## Publications

### Magazines

*Backpacker*
    (annual gear guide, March issue)
Rodale Publishing
33 East Minor Street
Emmaus, PA 18098
800-666-3434
www.bpbasecamp.com

*Bicycling*
    (annual gear guide, April issue)
Rodale Publishing
P.O. Box 7308
Red Oak, IA 51591
800-666-2806
www.bicycling.com

*Canoe & Kayak* (annual gear guide, December issue)
P.O. 3146
Kirkland, WA 98083
800-829-3340
www.canoeandkayak.com

*Outside*
   (annual buyer's guide, spring issue)
400 Market Street
Santa Fe, NM 87501
505-989-7100
www.outsidemag.com

**Directories**
Trailer Life Campground Directory
Good Sam Club/T.L. Enterprises Inc.
P.O. Box 6885
Englewood, CO 80155
800-234-3450
www.goodsamclub.com

Woodall's Campground Directory
P.O. Box 8600
Ventura, CA 93002
800-323-9076
www.woodalls.com

Don Wright's Guide to Free Campgrounds
Cottage Publications Inc.
24396 Pleasant View Drive
Elkhart, IN 46517
800-272-5518
www.cottagepub.com

# MINIMUM-IMPACT CAMPING

Carefree camping is careful camping—a mindset that encourages care for the land. For people to continue to enjoy wild lands, or even ordinary outdoor places, they should welcome the challenge to keep natural lands as close to their natural state as possible.

As more people have chosen to spend time in wilderness areas, more attention has been given to how that use affects the land. Attention has given way to recommendations for use, and while a few campers initially resented the perceived intrusion on "their" territory, most eventually have become conservation converts. "It's for your own good" is more than a convenient cliché—even children who would ordinarily balk at that blanket explanation will understand how it applies to the natural world they enjoy when camping.

It doesn't take an eco-scientist to see that wild

land can't stay wild if too much careless use disrupts its wildness. We shouldn't need a concerned naturalist to point out what should be so obvious: if we damage soil, plants cannot grow; if we cut down forests, we cut into all forest life; if we overabuse any land or water resources, the day will come when we won't be able to use them at all.

Careful camping is a conscious effort to minimize human impact on wild lands. While no impact is the ideal, the more realistic start is low or minimal impact.

We all know pollution is a bad word, but too often we connect it to the chemical hazards of industrial waste and acid rain—situations seemingly out of our control. But we do have control over other things. Think about the soap you use, the water you waste, or the litter you drop. Think about how noise pollutes the serenity of nature, how gaudy colors might destroy a landscape. Think about the campfire: once the center of camping life, now the center of controversy, sitting on an environmental fence, with convincing arguments on both sides.

Limitations or recommendations on use should not discourage new campers, but rather should encourage them to look for ways to achieve noimpact: it is for everyone's own good. Learn about the special considerations of each place you plan to visit, so you'll know what to do and what to avoid. Get involved with conservation groups and with other campers, so you can exchange ideas and ideals with people of like mind. Contact the National Outdoor Leadership School (NOLS) for information about their courses, which teach wilderness skills in locations around the world (see page 157).

"Leave No Trace" is the philosophy behind—

# Camping Mindset

Remember to practice minimum-impact camping.

- Try to walk on hard ground to avoid stepping on undergrowth that would be damaged.
- Camp where the ground is most durable; wear moccasins or sneakers around camp.
- Where a wilderness site is just beginning to show use, leave it alone so it has a chance to regrow. If possible, find another campsite.
- In a high-use area, stay in a site that is already impacted, to save the remaining land.
- Don't wear down paths around the campsite; vary your walking patterns.
- Try to camp at the time of year when you'd do the least damage. (For example, stay away from springtime wet trails.)
- Go camping in the off season sometime; fewer people, less impact.
- Pick a campsite by how well you can hide it; don't intrude on other campers' views.
- Use your radio for a five-minute weather broadcast, then put it away. Don't intrude on nature's sounds.
- Keep soap use to a minimum.

Biodegradables do break down more quickly than other soaps, but can still have a short-term impact on an area.
- Bathe away from the water source so soapy water can be filtered before returning to the stream or lake.
- Burn or carry out leftover food; don't bury it.
- While cleanup once meant "pick up your own mess," today you're asked to pick up any mess you see. Though annoying in principle, the alternative of leaving trash is unacceptable. Hope that your example will rub off.
- As government cuts back funding for wild lands, there is more need for volunteer help. Both the National Park Service and the USDA National Forests have volunteer programs; write for information. (Addresses and phone numbers are on page 151.)
- Also, watch newspapers for the date of a beach cleanup. Volunteer for an afternoon of picking up litter, then camp nearby and enjoy the beach. (Or call the Center for Marine Conservation for information; address and phone on page 151.)
- Never feed wild animals; try not

to disturb them in any way. Stay away from bird-nesting sites and turtle-hatching beaches.
- Check regulations for wilderness areas where you plan to camp. There may be limits on how long you can stay, or how many people can camp, as well as restrictions on fire use.
- Don't remove any artifacts you may find. If they're on public land, they're protected by law.
- In the national parks, and some other public lands, it is illegal to remove any natural objects—including flowers and plants.
- Backcountry camping is usually free, but you may need a fire permit and/or permission to camp. Call the land owner or managing agency.
- Continue your camping practices at home: use green products, recycle wherever possible, and use water sparingly at all times. Use your camping experiences to teach your children about the wonders of nature and the necessity of preserving the wilderness for future generations; in later years, they'll be able to make informed decisions on conservation and development issues.

and the name of—a program that teaches ways to protect the environment. The specific goal of the organization is to promote responsible use of wild lands by hikers and canoeists, but the ideas can prompt an attitude equally applicable in any outdoor surrounding.

The principles of Leave No Trace are:

1. Plan ahead and prepare.
2. Travel and camp on durable surfaces.
3. Dispose of waste properly.
4. Leave what you find.
5. Minimize campfire impacts.
6. Respect wildlife.
7. Be considerate of other visitors.

For more information, contact Leave No Trace, Inc. at 800-332-4100 or www.lnt.org.

If you can think in terms of "invisible" and "weightless," and then act as though you were, you'll be practicing minimum-impact camping, without putting a damper on the appreciation for, and the fun of, the outdoors.

# USEFUL ADDRESSES

For information on government lands:

National Park Service Information
Department of the Interior
1849 C Street, N.W., Room 1013
Washington, DC 20242
202-208-4747
www.nps.gov

National Park Service Trails
P.O. Box 37127
Washington, DC 20013-7127
202-208-4290
www.nps.gov/trails

National Wildlife Refuges
U.S. Fish and Wildlife Service
4401 North Fairfax Street
Arlington, VA 22203
800-344-WILD (800-344-9453)
www.refuges.fws.gov

U.S. Army Corps of Engineers Publications
    Depot
Regional Brochures
2803 52nd Avenue
Hyattsville, MD 20781-1102
301-394-0081
www.usace.army.mil/recreation
www.reserveusa.com

U.S.D.A. Forest Service
Public Affairs Office
National Headquarters
P.O. Box 96090
Washington, DC 20090-6090
202-205-1760
www.fs.fed.us/

U.S. Department of the Interior
Bureau of Land Management
Washington, DC 20240-0001
202-452-5125 (or look under the Bureau of Land
    Management in each state)
www.blm.gov

For information on conservation and environmental protection:

Center for Marine Conservation (CMC)
1725 DeSales Street N.W.
Suite 600
Washington, DC 20036
202-429-5609
www.cmc-ocean.org

Leave No Trace, Inc.
P.O. Box 997
Boulder, CO 80306
800-332-4100; 303-442-8222
www.lnt.org

National Audubon Society
700 Broadway
New York, NY 10003
212-979-3000
www.audubon.org

National Outdoor Leadership School (NOLS)
288 Main Street
Lander, WY 82520-3140
307-332-5300
www.nols.edu

National Wildlife Federation
1100 Wildlife Center Drive
Reston, VA 20190
800-822-9919
www.nwf.org

The Nature Conservancy
4245 N. Fairfax Drive, Suite 100
Arlington, VA 22203
800-628-6860
www.tnc.org

Sierra Club
85 2nd Street, 2nd floor
San Francisco, CA 94105-3441
415-977-5000
www.sierraclub.org

The Wilderness Society
1615 M Street, N.W.
Washington, DC 20036
202-833-2300

# APPENDIX: COOKOUT FOODS

With all the cooking methods available, most ordinary meals can be fixed outdoors. Camp cooking shouldn't rely on detailed instructions. You already know which foods go together by taste or tradition; start with familiar combinations, then try some new things, but do it one dish at a time. Children, especially, may not be excited about something different, so experiment in the backyard campground first. If successful, you'll add variety to your camping meals, plus you'll be able to time the outdoor cooking more accurately.

For each camping trip, make two lists: one, a menu of what you plan to eat at each meal (plus snacks); and two, the itemized list of what you'll need to prepare those meals. Arrange the menu according to which items should be eaten first (depending on how long foods will keep), which ones start frozen, which ones involve planning ahead (like marinating meat or soaking beans).

For the cook-ahead-and-freeze meals, use large cans for freezing. The frozen food acts as an ice block for a while; when you're ready to eat, heat the food right in the can, then recycle the can. The more food you pack frozen, the less ice you need to buy.

Plan for backup cooking methods. If you can't have a campfire because of rain or regulations, or if your propane grill quits for reasons unknown, be ready with a cookstove, even if it's only a single-burner.

## WAKE-UP FOOD

### FISHERMAN'S SLUMGULLION

*Approximate amounts for four:*
**4 to 6 slices bacon (or ham or sausage); or use mushrooms, for a meatless version**
**2 large potatoes**
**1 medium onion**
**½ green pepper (optional)**
**6 eggs, scrambled with a bit of milk**
**4 slices cheese (your favorite kind)**
**Salt and pepper, if desired**

Cut the meat into bite-size pieces and brown in frying pan. (If bacon, remove excess fat.) Dice or slice potatoes and brown with sliced onions. When cooked, add diced green pepper; pour in scrambled egg mixture, and when partially set, lay cheese slices on top. Cover with lid or foil. When cheese melts, eggs should be set; cut into serving pieces, and serve with toast, biscuits, cornbread, or bread and butter.

(Good at lunch or dinnertime, too.)

### SUNNYSIDE SANDWICHES

If nothing else, fast-food breakfasts are easy to prepare and neat to eat. Copy the restaurants' ideas: serve fried eggs and cheese with ham, sausage, or bacon on any kind of bread, bun, bagel, biscuit, or muffin. Yours will be better.

- Out of bacon? Sprinkle bacon bits, or slice a bit of summer sausage or pepperoni.
- Out of fresh cheese? Use cheese spread, if you have some along.
- No ham? Open a can of Spam (it's better hot).

## HASHWICH

Some campers object to corned beef hash, just because it bears an unfortunate resemblance to dog food. If you can get past that association, cut a ½-inch-thick slice of hash; fry or grill one side, flip it over, and break an egg on top (dent the hash first). Put a lid over the top so the egg cooks. Use it in a sandwich, or eat as is, with toast or muffins on the side.

## HOT FIBER

Though the easiest breakfast to carry and prepare, hot cereals are seldom the number one favorite, so get creative with toppings: offer a choice and let everyone add their own.

- Butter and cinnamon sugar
- Honey or maple syrup
- Brown sugar and raisins
- Jam or preserves
- Fresh, canned, or dried fruit
- Crumbled bacon
- Dates and nuts
- Wheat germ or wheat bran

## COLD FLAKES OR GRANOLA

There may be nothing outdoorsy about cold cereal, but if you add enough fruit and nuts, it can be a semi-healthful tummy filler. Try mixing some uncooked rolled oats with the family's favorite packaged cereals, then let everyone toss in their choice of:

- Banana slices
- Berries
- Canned or fresh peaches
- Raisins
- Dates, apricots, prunes
- Nuts
- Wheat germ or wheat bran
- Trail mix

## GRIDDLE CAKES

Even if you seldom eat pancakes at home, you will at camp. Use a packaged mix or bring your own basic baking mix—and be prepared to mix extra.

*Basic mix:*
**4 cups flour (use all-purpose, or substitute 1 cup whole wheat)**
**3 tablespoons baking powder**
**1 teaspoon salt**
**¼ cup sugar**
**1 cup instant nonfat milk**

Mix and store in airtight container.
To make 8 to 10 pancakes, combine:
**1¼ cups basic mix**
**1 egg**
**¾ cup water**
**1 tablespoon butter or margarine, melted**

Drop spoonfuls of batter onto a hot frying pan or griddle; bake till bubbles appear, then flip and brown the other side.

For variation, add any of the following to the pancake batter: wheat germ (or wheat or oat bran), sliced strawberries or bananas, blueberries, cinnamon and nuts.

*Put on top of pancakes:*
- Syrup (maple, fruit, whatever)
- Cinnamon sugar or brown sugar
- Jam
- Diced canned fruit with syrup
- Apple butter
- Honey

*Alternative pancakes:*
Make corn cakes, by substituting cornmeal for half the flour in your recipe—or, easier yet, get a packaged cornbread mix that can be adapted to pancakes (Jiffy brand comes to mind).

# Meal Ideas and Tips

## Breakfast

- Fry bacon slices on aluminum foil. Poke a few holes in the foil to allow fat to drip. Or, cook bacon on a skewer. Poke a hole in one end of the bacon slice and wrap it around the skewer. Secure the other end, and roast over coals. (Cook ham and sausage directly on the grill, with or without a foil lining.)
- Fry or scramble eggs in a frying pan, "just like home."
- Use a metal canning jar ring, or a tuna can with top and bottom removed, to poach or fry an egg for a circular sandwich.
- Use leftover meats and vegetables for breakfast omelets: ham, bacon, smoked sausage, ground beef, green pepper, mushrooms, onions, zucchini. Cheese becomes an extra.
- Toast bread or buns: on foil over the fire; in a frying pan on the stove; on a "flame tamer" (a metal ring that diffuses the flame) over the fire. Campers' "pyramid" toasters must be watched carefully; bread may dry to crouton texture or char beyond edibility.
- When toasting bread in a pan, weigh down the bread with a coffee mug, and it will toast faster. (Use a pan with non-stick coating.)
- Each person can toast a piece of bread on a fork over coals, like marshmallows—fun and deliciously smoky.
- Pancakes cook faster on a large griddle, the kind that fits over both burners of a typical camp stove.
- Make syrup with sugar and water. To 1 cup sugar (all white, or half white, half brown) add ¼ cup of boiling water, and stir till the sugar dissolves. Add a teaspoon of maple flavoring, or a dash of cinnamon, and boil a few more minutes. Add sugar or water if needed for proper consistency.
- For a filling breakfast, try toasted bagels with butter and jam, honey, peanut butter, or cream cheese, with bacon or ham on top or alongside.
- Try a favorite hobo/hunter/Boy Scout and probably pioneer tip: Mix a basic biscuit dough really thick, and wrap it around a stick to bake over coals. Spread with butter and jam or honey.
- Fresh fruit—sliced and served alone, or diced in cereal—adds a true country flavor to camp breakfast.

## Beverages

- Take instant milk for baking, and serve it with cereal, too. (You won't have room in the cooler for large containers of fresh milk.)
- To make the mixed milk more palatable, or at least acceptable, add a bit of vanilla extract. Start with ½ teaspoon per quart and taste it; real vanilla has a stronger flavor than you might think.
- Coffee singles (real coffee in a bag) are the most convenient form for camp coffee, and may be an acceptable substitute for fresh-brewed coffee.
- Or, brew individual cups of coffee using Melitta paper filters with a "drip" funnel. (Pre-grind your favorite beans.)
- Alternate with flavored teas (by the bag) or cocoa (by the envelope). Or, try a cup of hot beef bouillon some chilly morning; it's almost as good as caffeine for your wake-up start.
- Make lemonade, limeade, or other frozen juice with seltzer instead of plain water for a good soda compromise.

## Lunch and Dinner

- At home, fix a whole beef roast, or bake a ham or turkey breast. At camp, just slice or dice for lunches or dinner meals.
- If you miscalculate the deli order (or your family's appetites), have a backup. Cans of chunk ham, chicken, salmon, or tuna can be mixed with condiments of your choice (try pickle relish, mayo, and minced onion) to serve on bread or crackers. Add canned tuna to a macaroni salad for a lunch or dinner meal. Crackers with cheese spreads are also good for a lunchtime fill-in.
- Mix a can of cheese soup into some cooked macaroni for a quick mac-and-cheese lunch. Add hot dogs or ham chunks and diced onion and green pepper for a main meal.
- Slide kabobbed food into a pita pocket, or roll it in a tortilla and call it a fajita. Kabob cooking is one way to be sure children get veggies on their plate. Getting them from plate to mouth is another story.
- Your family's favorite potato, pasta, and egg salads will be a good complement to any grilled foods. Cook the potatoes, pasta, and eggs at home; at camp, mix the salads as you need them. Add chopped fresh vegetables

# Meal Ideas and Tips (continued)

and chunks of grilled chicken or fish to your favorite shape pasta.

- Check the farm stands on the way to the campground for fresh fruits and vegetables in season.

## Snacks

- Make your own trail mix. Pick a combination of dried fruits, nuts, seeds, and other high-energy snacks from the bins at a health food store or bulk food section of some supermarkets. A personal favorite (not very exotic, but always tasty) combines banana chips, assorted nuts and seeds, raisins, and apricots.
- Buy an assortment of dried fruit in bulk from a health food store. It will be cheaper than the packaged supermarket variety, and probably fresher and tastier, too.
- Bring granola bars. Look for the original oats-nuts-and-honey type, not the chocolate-covered variety that pass for candy bars.

- Low-salt, low-fat whole-wheat crackers are good plain or any way.
- Cookies and candy can stave off a sweet attack, *if* you can keep them hidden so they're available for emergency consumption.

## Desserts

- If you have some kind of oven, you can make individual pineapple upside-down cakes, using recycled tuna cans. Grease the cans, put a pineapple slice in the bottom of each, and sprinkle with brown sugar. Fill the cans with yellow or white cake batter, and bake.
- Buy a regular cake mix that requires three eggs. Divide the mix into thirds so you can bake only one-third of the mix. This amount fits nicely into a small frying pan; it bakes fairly quickly at low heat. Use a thick aluminum pan with a flame tamer, if necessary. Grease and flour the pan.

- Anyone with the will (and the ingredients) can make any kind of pie by baking it in a metal (or disposable foil) pie plate inside a Dutch oven.
- Individual yogurt cups, with fresh fruit added, are as good as ice cream (almost) and probably healthier, too.
- Make instant puddings from mix and instant milk. Pour into graham cracker tart shells, and sprinkle coconut on top.
- Lazy-day dessert: pudding cups straight from the supermarket cooler to camp.
- Lots of no-cook dessert mixes are available, too.
- When it's watermelon season, dessert's already made. Eat fresh-cut slices, or convince someone to cut bite-size pieces of melon so you can mix it with other fruit in a giant salad that could be dinner itself, with a side dish of cottage cheese.

## QUICK BAKES

For Sunday morning coffeecake, use any packaged baking mix. Put the dough in a foil cake pan, if baking in a reflector oven; or put it in a heavy frying pan to bake (covered) over a low flame on stove or campfire. Sprinkle with topping (mix everything till it's crumbly) before baking.

*Coffeecake topping:*
**¼ cup brown sugar**
**½ teaspoon cinnamon**
**1 tablespoon margarine or butter**
**1 tablespoon flour**
**A few chopped nuts (optional)**

Or, bake the coffeecake plain, then decorate with swirls of "frosting"—maple syrup or honey mixed with confectioner's sugar to a spreadable consistency.

To make muffins, start with the same basic batter; vary the recipe with different additions, such as:

- Bananas and nuts (mash the banana)
- Blueberries
- Raisins, diced apricots, or other dried fruit
- Diced fresh apples and cinnamon
- Or, replace some of the liquid with orange juice and some rind (zest).

To bake muffins without a muffin tin, mix the batter on the thick side, drop large spoonfuls onto a greased and floured frying pan, cover and bake over a low flame. (They'll pull apart after baking.)

# LUNCH AND MUNCH

### STACK-A-SANDWICH

Often, camp lunch is a do-it-yourself meal, so think like a sub shop, where "fixins" make the sandwich. Start with hard rolls or dark rye bread; stack on deli cold cuts or your own home-roasted beef, turkey, chicken, or ham. Add some cheese slices, then dress up the sandwich with lettuce leaves and tomato slices; onion and green pepper rings; alfalfa sprouts, avocado or olive slices, sweet or hot peppers; mayo, mustard, or oil and vinegar sprinkles.

To go with the sandwiches, keep a cooler container filled with bite-size celery, carrots, pepper, broccoli, cauliflower, radishes. When the fresh stuff's gone, serve pickles (dill or sweet) or olives (green or black) and chips, if you must (shoestring potatoes pack smallest).

### STUFF-A-SANDWICH

Use the cooked fish left over from last night's dinner (in lieu of tuna for a tuna salad) to make a sandwich filling for pita pockets. Vegetables-only are good in whole-wheat pitas. You can use practically anything, hot or cold, to stuff a pita.

### HOTWICH

On a chilly camp day, think hot sandwiches. Put together an appropriate combination (ham and cheese with green pepper; beef with onion; salami, cheese, and tomato) and grill, fry, or toast them wrapped in foil.

### CAMPFIRE CLASSIC

Have a hot dog/frankfurter/wiener:

*Basic:* dog on bun with mustard or horseradish, ketchup, relish, and diced onion.

*New York:* dog on bun with sauerkraut and your choice of "other."

*Mexican:* dog on bun with chili or salsa and maybe grated cheese on top.

*Cheese:* dog split lengthwise with cheese in middle (use flavored cheeses like bacon, smoke, garlic, caraway).

*Uptown dogs:* Buy knockwurst, bratwurst, kielbasa to vary the flavor and texture of hot dog meals.

COLEMAN COMPANY, INC.

*Turkey dogs:* Look for smoked sausage that's made with turkey, so you won't feel guilty about all that fat. For an Italian turkey dog, top the sandwich with sliced onion and green pepper strips, and steam/cook in a foil package.

## SKEWERED DOGS

Cut any type of sausage into 1-inch pieces and alternate on skewers with pineapple chunks and anything else that sounds good to you. Baste with pineapple juice and a bit of Dijon mustard as the sausage cooks.

## MEXICAN CAMP

If you have time and ambition, fix tacos. Make up your own filling: ground beef, pork, or turkey with chili powder in tomato sauce. Use refried beans, or your own bean-based chili for a no-meat version. Cook the filling at home and freeze it to save cooking time at camp.

Grate some cheese, chop some vegetables (lettuce, tomato, onion, pepper—whatever you have and whatever sounds good). Heat the taco shells at fireside for a few minutes, stuff them, and garnish with sour cream, guacamole, salsa—whatever's in the cooler.

## SOUP FOR LUNCH

Instant soups and cup-a-soups are handy hand and tummy warmers.

# MAIN MEALS

### KABOBBING

Cooked over campfire or grill, kabobs are relatively easy for the cook and really easy for the dishwasher, since they are, in effect, one-pot meals without the pot.

Some campers shy away from skewer cooking, complaining that certain items burn while others don't cook well. That's a problem with an easy solution: either precook the slower-cooking foods, like onions or potatoes (boil small red potatoes in skin, and leave skin on when skewering), or use separate skewers for separate timing. Skewer pork and shrimp separately, pork because it takes a longer time to cook, shrimp because it takes *less* time than most vegetables.

For the most flavorful kabobs, marinate meat at least an hour (longer if the marinade is a tenderizer, too) and baste meat and vegetables while cooking. Oil-and-vinegar salad dressing is a simple but tasty marinade. Or use olive oil, garlic, and fresh-squeezed lemon, lime, or orange juice. Soy sauce and garlic (maybe with ginger, too) makes an easy teriyaki marinade.

### KABOB COMBOS

- Beef (sirloin), chicken (white meat chunks), or lamb with onion sections, green pepper chunks, cherry tomatoes, mushroom caps (potatoes optional).
- Pork tenderloin, sliced zucchini, green pepper, onion, mushrooms.
- Pork or ham, pineapple, mushrooms, potatoes.
- Any type of sausage, like knockwurst or kielbasa, can be used with your choice of veggies.
- Delete the meat from any of the above, and you probably won't even miss it.

In theory, you could try a different kabob combo every time; in practice, people tend to repeat a few favorites.

### REAL BEEF

The easiest cut of beef to cook is individual steaks, grilled to individual taste (or close).

London broil is another favorite; it takes longer to cook, but sometimes you'll have leftovers for the next day's lunch. This meat benefits from a tenderizing marinade, while steaks require nothing but sometimes get a massive coating of mixed spices.

As with all grilling, cooking times for beef vary according to the thickness of the meat, the heat of the coals, and how close the grill is to the heat. Guess timing for cooking it rare or well done on the basis of backyard barbecues, plus some extra.

### CAMPBURGERS

Hamburgers are almost a requisite camp meal. Vary the toppings; now's your chance to try all the combos you've seen on restaurant menus. Use different cheeses: cheddar, Swiss, mozzarella, blue, feta. Add mushroom slices, onions (grilled or raw), pepper rings, bacon, olives. Top with salsa or pizza sauce.

## CAMP RIBS

At the recommended 1 pound per person, actual spareribs take way too much room in a cooler. But outdoors is the place for barbecued ribs, so try to make space occasionally for a meal of back ribs (more meat per rib). At home, many cooks pre-boil ribs; this removes some fat, and the ribs stay juicier. Duplicate this at camp by foil-wrapping and steaming them for half an hour; then grill at low heat for another 30 or 40 minutes, brushing with barbecue sauce the last 20 minutes of cooking time. (Or, boil them at home, to shorten cooking time at camp.)

## ONE-POT MEALS

Stews, hearty soups, and chili are good bring-from-home meals to serve the first night at camp, or, if frozen, whenever they thaw. To cook these at camp, use the Dutch oven—or heat them in the same coffee can used for freezing (heat carefully so the bottom doesn't burn).

## CHICKEN ON THE GRILL

After hamburgers and hot dogs, grilled chicken is a popular cookout meal, so why not bring it to camp, too? Place chicken pieces on the grill and cook 10 minutes; turn and cook the other side 10 minutes; then repeat, both sides (total cooking time 40 minutes). Adjust the timing for larger pieces. During the last half of the cooking time, baste with a sauce of choice:

- Standard barbecue sauce, with or without your additions.
- Herbed butters—melted butter with your choice of herbs.
- Soy sauce and ginger.

## CORNISH HENS

Though readily available, Cornish hens seem like a special treat. Cut the birds in half lengthwise and marinate for an hour or so in a mixture of soy sauce (½ cup), honey (2 or 3 tablespoons), garlic, and ground ginger to taste.

Set the hens on the grill, skin-side up, and cover loosely with foil for the first half of the cooking, so they steam as much as broil (the hens don't have much fat to keep them moist). Baste with the marinade; turn the hens three times, like the chicken pieces described above, so cooking on each side is done in two stages. They'll probably take the same time to cook as the chicken. (If you're not fond of soy sauce, use a marinade of your choice; Cornish hens are also good plain, or basted with herbed butter.)

## ROAST-A-DUCK

Some day when you feel like a frontierperson, cook a duck. Spit roasting is the most practical, whether on a propane grill or over a charcoal or wood fire (be aware, though, that this last option could take all afternoon and a lot of charcoal or wood).

Poke a bunch of holes in the skin; ducks have a lot of fat, and it needs many avenues of escape. Wire the duck securely to the spit. When it's perfectly done, it will be crispy and brown outside, and tender and juicy inside. The only bad part: one duck doesn't go too far; estimates are to allow 1 to 1½ pounds per person.

## STIR-STEAMED CHICKEN

Use the campfire to cook an oriental dinner, without a wok. Wrap chunks of chicken and your choice of vegetables in foil packets (together or separately, according to cooking times). To each packet, add sauce or spices and a bit of water to steam flavor through the food. Set the foil packs on a grill or over coals; when ready to serve, spoon the contents over rice or oriental noodles. Surprise everybody with fortune cookies.

## CAMPER'S CORDON BLEU

To prove that campers do not live by hot dogs alone, fix Chicken Cordon Bleu for some special occasion celebration.

Sauté slices of boneless chicken breast; for each serving, sandwich thin slices of smoked ham and a slice of Swiss cheese between two pieces of chicken. Roll the "sandwich" in flour, egg, and breadcrumbs; sauté it in a frying pan on the camp stove, or bake on a foil-covered grill.

## CAST-IRON CHICKEN

If you're a cast-iron cooker, you may want to fry some chicken. No doubt other pans will work, but the cast iron retains heat best. Put breading mix into a plastic bag, and shake the chicken pieces inside to coat them; then fry as usual.

## ALTERNATE FOWL

Substitute turkey for any chicken meal; either cut it into smaller pieces, or adjust the cooking time.

# Cooking Ideas and Tips

- Top home-cooked stew with camp-cooked dumplings.
- Serve home-cooked chili with shredded cheese, diced onion, and cornbread on the side.
- Toward the end of cooking, brush a Cornish hen or duckling with a 2-to-1 mix of fruit preserves (apricot or peach) and honey.
- For a quick coleslaw, shred cabbage; make carrot strips with a vegetable peeler. Add thinly sliced onion, and hold it together with mayo or oil-and-vinegar dressing. Or, shred a small head of red cabbage. Add dressing made with ½ cup mayo, 2 tablespoons cider vinegar, salt, pepper, and dill.
- Soak corn-on-the-cob (silk removed, but still wrapped in its husk) in water for an hour before putting it on coals or grill. "Bake" for about a half hour.
- Steam any vegetable for 10 to 15 minutes in a foil packet with a few tablespoons of water. (You can vary by substituting an oil-and-vinegar dressing for half the water.)
- Put thickly sliced vegetables directly on the grill; cover them loosely with foil, and cook till tender.
- Foil-wrap baking potatoes (the red ones stay moister) or sweet potatoes, and bake them in hot coals for about an hour. Poke with fork before wrapping to allow steam to escape.
- Cut fresh potatoes into spears; add salt, pepper, and spices, and put into oiled shallow baking dish at fireside, to "bake" while meat/chicken is cooking.
- With leftover mashed potatoes (or those freshly made with instant potato flakes), make pat-

ties. Dip them in flour and fry (in bacon fat, if you made bacon). *Variations:* Add a bit of minced onion, some parsley, some grated cheese. Serve with sour cream or plain yogurt.

## Baked Beans

Some afternoon when you have nothing else to do, make a pot of baked beans:

*Real Baked Beans*
1 pound navy beans
1 large onion, diced
¼ cup vegetable oil
¼ cup each brown sugar, molasses, maple syrup
1 teaspoon each salt, dry mustard
Black pepper to taste

Cover beans with water and soak overnight. Drain water. Combine all ingredients in heavyweight bean pot and add boiling water to cover. Put on lid and bake in home oven or simmer over campfire for 5 hours at low heat. Remove lid and cook 1 more hour.

*Quick Baked Beans*
1 15-ounce can pork-and-beans (or porkless)
1 15-ounce can kidney beans
1 small onion, chopped
¼ to ½ teaspoon mustard
⅓ cup brown sugar
4 slices bacon, cut into pieces (optional)

Combine ingredients and simmer at least an hour.

## Rice

- Basic rice: Dice and brown some onions in a pan. Add water, bring to a boil, add rice.

- Add any combination of celery, carrots, green pepper, mushrooms (use the stems you removed when skewering the caps).
- Almonds or walnuts (or other nuts/seeds) add good taste and texture.
- Dissolve chicken, beef, or vegetable bouillon in the cooking water.
- Choose your spices to complement what you're serving.
- Shake on some soy sauce for a stronger flavor with kabobs or barbecue.
- Add diced tomatoes and a can of black beans, or some shredded cabbage, for a vegetarian main meal. Or, try shell beans; any kind of cooked beans, especially chickpeas; tofu; mung sprouts; water chestnuts; roasted Spanish chestnuts; any kind of grated cheese—combine your family's favorites.
- For Spanish rice, use tomato juice (or sauce) for part of the liquid; add onions and green pepper, chili powder, and tomato chunks.
- To any of the above, add canned chunk ham, chicken, or tiny shrimp. Call it fried rice (toss in a scrambled egg or two for authenticity), and you have dinner.

Turkey burgers need taste boosters. Try onion and parsley, or herbs and seasonings of your choice. Bacon on top is good, but it would probably destroy the cholesterol-cutting benefit of the turkey burgers.

Smoked turkey sausage does a good job of hiding the fact that it's supposed to be healthier: it still tastes like "real" (beef/pork) sausage. Chop the sausages into sections and sauté with onion and pepper rings, to serve over rice.

## ONTARIO FISHING GUIDE'S SHORE LUNCH

This lunch is really dinner. Save up your fried food quota so you can enjoy it guiltlessly.

Prepare pickerel fillets for frying (or use whatever you caught); dip them in flour, egg ,and bread crumbs, seasoned with salt and pepper.

Fry some bacon in a well-seasoned cast-iron frying pan (drain and save the fat).

Slice some potatoes (peeled or not) and fry them in the bacon fat; toss in a few circles of sliced onion, too.

Fast-fry the fish, also in bacon fat (or *some* bacon fat, some vegetable oil).

Sprinkle lemon juice on the fish; you don't need tartar sauce with your super-fresh fish. Serve the fish with the potatoes, baked beans, and bread or biscuits, and eat all you can.

*Per-person guesstimates:*
2 bacon slices
1 medium potato
2 to 5 pieces of fish, depending on size of fish
    and appetite
Onion slices, lemon to taste

# Cooking Tips and Food Safety

- Wrap meats or vegetables in cabbage leaves before enclosing in a foil package to steam/cook.
- Don't poke a fork into meat as it's cooking; it will lose juices and get dry.
- Don't flatten burgers, for the same reason.
- When grilling with skewers, remember to use the right kind of metal skewers, those with an angular shape so food turns with the skewer. If you use bamboo skewers, soak them in water first. Enlist aid in chopping food to skewer size (1-inch to 1½-inch cubes, slices, or pieces). Older children can help, with small, serrated knives.
- Alter prepared barbecue sauce to your taste preference: add more onion or garlic; brown sugar, honey, molasses; or chili powder, other spices, hot sauce.
- Foil-wrap country-style ribs with some barbecue sauce. Eat as is for dinner, or thinly slice the meat for jumbo barbecue sandwiches.

- Steaks and burgers need a hot fire; ribs and chops need a slow fire so meat cooks through without burning outside. To test temperature: Put your hand about 4 inches above coals. If you can't leave it there, it's a hot fire. If your hand is still there after 5 seconds, it's a low heat.
- If you're shaping hamburger patties at camp, use a sandwich bag or waxed paper to handle meat. (It's hard to wash hands without warm water.)
- To prevent flare-ups, cut excess fat from steaks or chops.
- To prevent meat from curling, score the layer of fat lining the steak.
- To prevent sticking, rub some fat from the steak onto the grill. (Or spray with non-stick coating, if you packed it.)
- If a garage sale or flea market search turns up a cast-iron frying pan with ridges on the bottom, buy it for frying fish.
- Don't put the cooked burgers,

chicken, or ribs on the plate where the raw meat was, since hot water is not immediately accessible for in-between washing.
- Don't leave food out of the cooler any longer than necessary.
- Be sure food is thoroughly cooked: no pink chicken or pork.
- Try to keep hot things hot, cold cold.
- Signs of food poisoning (badly upset stomach with flu-like symptoms) usually show up a few hours after eating the problem food, and can last for a few hours or a few days. If symptoms are more severe (difficulty in swallowing or breathing, double vision, or other indication that the nervous system is affected) or if the person is young, old, pregnant, or already ill, find a doctor.

## HONEY-FRIED FISH

While you're still in fish-fry mode, try another way; this is particularly good with bass.

Use fish fillets about the thickness of your hand. Mix 2 eggs with 2 tablespoons of honey (or maple syrup) and a bit of water. Dip the fish to cover well; best is to let the fish soak a bit in the egg mixture.

Dip the pieces in a half-and-half mix of flour and bread crumbs.

Place a cast-iron pan over the heat; when it's good and hot, add butter or oil, pop the fish in, and sauté it "quick-quick." The fish will be brown and crisp, and oh so tasty.

## BARBECUED SHRIMP

If you're camping near shrimping waters, get some fresh shrimp to cook on the grill. Skewers help keep the shrimp *on* the grill. Cook the shrimp just until they turn pink.

*For marinade and basting:*

- Soy sauce and vegetable oil, with pineapple juice or ginger.
- Olive oil, lemon juice, and garlic (or oil-and-vinegar salad dressing).

## STEAM HEAT

Instead of cutting a larger fish into frying-size pieces, bake or steam/poach it. Place skinned fillets in a foil wrapper (double thickness on the bottom). Then add some liquid and spices. The combinations for steaming mixtures are endless; keep experimenting until you find those you like best. Remember, though, that fish has a fairly delicate flavor, so if you want to taste fish, go easy on the stronger spices.

To cook the fish, seal the foil package and set it on the grill. Peek from time to time to check progress; cooking will probably take from half an hour to 45 minutes, perhaps more if a very thick fish. (It's done if it flakes readily when poked with a fork.)

*Flavoring possibilities:*

- Onion, butter, oregano
- Butter, paprika, sour cream
- Dill, lemon, and butter
- Celery, onion, parsley
- Mushrooms, green onion, parsley
- Lemon juice, bay leaf, pepper
- Any cream soup
- White wine

## GRILLED FISH

If you have a fine-meshed grill or screen to put over the campfire or charcoal grill, you can broil fish directly over the fire. Rub the cooking surface with oil to prevent sticking, and baste the fish with herbed butter as it cooks.

Larger fish steaks can be marinated and broiled. Make a marinade of ¼ cup each vegetable oil and vinegar, 2 tablespoons soy sauce, and a minced garlic clove. Soak fish for an hour, and grill.

Some fish has a stronger flavor than you'd like, even when freshly caught. Grill it with a honey-based barbecue sauce. Sounds odd, but it makes a great fish sandwich.

# SWEET TREATS

### MELLOW MALLOWS

Toasted marshmallows might be addictive. Luckily, you can toast them over a home stove if it's ever really necessary—though the ambiance will never equal the warmth of glowing embers, with the aroma of woodsmoke and the hiss of bubbling sugar.

Marshmallows roasting on the ends of freshly cut sticks may be a thing of the past, but marshmallows toasting on skewers (or even hot dog forks) taste just as good.

Toss some melted marshmallows onto a fruit salad—or make some s'mores.

### S'MORES

Standard Girl Scout fare, this is a dessert any camper wants some more of.

Start with a graham cracker, and lay a piece of a chocolate bar on top. Toast a marshmallow to your idea of perfection, and ease it off the stick and onto the chocolate. Top the sandwich with another graham cracker, and indulge. (Or, leave it open-faced and get really messy.)

Any extras in the chocolate bar (nuts, toffee, or crispy bits) will be welcome additions to the s'mores.

### SANDWICH PIES

If you have one of the two-sided pans for cooking hot sandwiches over a fire, you have an easy way to bake mini-pies. Your dough may masquerade as biscuit mix, and the filling come straight from a can, but it will all taste wonderful.

## HOT APPLES

For baked apples, remove the core and fill the void with any combination of: brown sugar or cinnamon sugar; raisins, dates, or crushed pineapple; nuts or butter. Wrap in foil, or put 4 or 6 apples in a baking tin and cover with foil. Bake until tender.

- Roast an apple on the end of a stick (or skewer or fork) till the skin splits, signifying it is cooked. Roll it in cinnamon sugar, and put it back on the fire for a minute till the sugar glazes. Cool it enough to eat some, then dip and roast again.

## FRUIT KABOBS

On small skewers, thread combinations of:

- Canned or fresh peaches, cut into sections
- Thick slices of banana
- Apple wedges
- Pineapple chunks (fresh is best)

Alternate fruit with some marshmallows. Grill and baste with pineapple juice, orange juice, or honey.

## BAKED BANANA

Peel a banana and cut it in half lengthwise; take out a wedge and fill the void with pineapple chunks; sprinkle on brown sugar or coconut flakes; wrap in the peel and in foil, and "bake" over the fire for 8 to 10 minutes.

Instead of pineapple, fill the banana with chocolate or butterscotch bits, mini-marshmallows, nuts, or whatever combination of goodies sounds good to you.

## FAKE FRUIT COBBLER

Use peaches, blueberries, raspberries, or apples, sliced and sugared where necessary. Put the fruit in a pan, either underneath or on top of a biscuit or shortcake dough. Either way, it will taste great after baking, even without a dollop of ice cream or whipped topping.

# A FEW CAMP-FOOD THOUGHTS

Put together a small spice kit of favorite seasonings. For a basic assortment, try garlic powder, oregano, basil, parsley, dill, chili powder, cinnamon, ginger, salt and pepper. You might also bring Worcestershire sauce, Tabasco sauce, soy sauce, honey, Parmesan cheese—and maybe some hardwood chips to use for a smoky flavor when grilling (see pages 101–2). Remember cooking/salad oil, vinegar, lemon juice, sugar, fresh garlic and onions (and dried onion and vegetable flakes). Sandwich condiments—mayo, ketchup, mustard, relish, and butter or margarine—will probably be on the cooler list.

Dehydrate your own vegetables for soups and stews, or fruits for cereal and snacks. (See page 127 and read *Trail Food* by Alan S. Kesselheim, Ragged Mountain Press, 1994, for ideas and strategies.)

Toss salads in a zip-top bag: no bowl to wash. Marinate meats and vegetables in a plastic zip-top bag, for the same reason.

At breakfast, fill a Thermos bottle with hot water so you can have a hot drink or instant soup at lunchtime without fire or stove use.

Stew or soak dried fruit at night for the next day's breakfast. In the evening, cook potatoes or pasta and eggs for the next day's lunch salads. (Cook the eggs in the same pot as the pasta.)

Heat a pot of water while you're eating breakfast or dinner so it's ready for washing dishes when you've finished your meal.

Keep food handy in the kitchen area of your campsite by day, but put it into the car (or otherwise secure from animals) at night, *not* in the tent. And no bedtime snacking: the distinct aroma of nacho tortilla chips carries a long way, and night creatures don't know if it comes from an empty or a full bag.

Take a small stash of canned food in case you aren't able to cook: ham, chicken chunks, salmon; potato and bean salads, beets, applesauce; fruit or pudding.

# INDEX

Numbers in **bold** refer to pages with illustrations

canoe camping, 123–**24**
  buying a canoe, 123, 147
  canoe maintenance and repair, 126, 139, 141
  equipment checklist for, 145
  paddling tips, **125**
  picking a campsite, 125–26
canopy tarps, 29–30, 31, 32, 138
careful camping, 149
cat holes, 50
chairs, **30–31**, 146
charcoal fires, 98–**99**, 100
checklists, equipment
  campers' needs, 144
  camp setup, 142–43
  canoe/boat, 145
  car, 145
  dog, 145
  first-aid, 79
  food preparation and storage, 143–44
  optional items, 144–45
  pack-and-go planner, 89
chipmunks, 45
citronella, 46, 78
clothing, about
  checklist for, 144
  discouraging bugs with, 74
  fabrics, 65
  layering, 63
  preventing sunburn with, 65, 72, **73**, 78
  using backpacks and duffel bags to carry, 67
  washing, 71
clothing, types of
  for backpacking, 129
  bottoms, 63
  for children, 64, 65
  footwear, 65, 66–**67**, 112
  gloves, 66
  hats, 64, 65, **73**
  for hiking, 112
  outerwear, **64**
  rain gear, 65, **66**
  sleepwear, 65
  tops, 63
Coleman camp fuel, 39
compasses, **114**, **116**, 146–47
conservation information, addresses for, 151
cook fires, about, 98
cook fires, types of
  charcoal, 98–99
  pit, 99, 100
  wood, 96–**97**
cooking. See also eating; food; recipes
  canopies, 32

as enjoyable element of camping, 94
  food safety precautions, 160
  ideas and tips, 100–101, 102, 159, 162
  organizing areas, 32
  safety precautions, 101
  selecting a site for, 22
  washing dishes, 109, 110–11
cooking, and fires
  barbecue grills, 101–2
  charcoal, 98–**99**, 100
  cooking platforms, **97**–98
  Dutch ovens, 99, 100, **101**, 103
  grills and spits, **97**–98, 100
  reflector ovens, **102**
  tripods, 96–**97**
  wind screens, **99**
cooking equipment
  cookware tips, 105
  coolers, 107–**8**, 139, 140–41
  dining ware, 104–6
  food containers, 105, 106
  keeping foods hot and cold, 107
  portable cabinets for, **106**
  portable refrigerators, 108
  pots and pans, 96, 100, 103–**4**
  toasters, 105
  utensils, **104**
cookstoves, two-burner, **94**–96
  maintaining, 95, 139, 140
  sources for, 147
coolers, 107–**8**, 139, 140–41
cots, 54, **55**, 58
cottonmouths, **77**
cuts, first aid for, 80

**D**
DEET-based repellents, 75, 78
desert camping, **130**
dessert
  ideas and tips, 154
  recipes, 161–62
dining ware, 104–6
dinner
  ideas and tips, 154–55, 159
  recipes, 157–58, 160, 161
dishes, washing, 109, 110–11
dogs as campers, 81–82, 83
  equipment checklist for, 145
dog ticks, **76**
dome tents
  advantages vs. disadvantages of, 14–**15**
  setting up, **25**, **26**
duffel bags, 67
Dutch ovens, 99, 100, **101**, 103

**E**
eating. See also cooking; cooking, and fires; cooking equipment; cookstoves, two-burner; food; recipes
  canopies for, 29–30, **34**
  selecting a site for, 22
  tables for, **32**
ehrlichiosis, 75
emergencies, preparing for, 116–17, 118
environmental protection information, addresses for, 151
eye injuries, first aid for, 80

**F**
family reunions, 122
filters, water, **110**
fires. See campfires; cook fires, about; cook fires, types of; cooking, and fires
fire starters, 35–36, 38, 117
firewood, 36, 38
first aid, 77, 79–80
fish hook injuries, first aid for, 80
flashlights, 40, 42–43
floors, tent, 18
flowerpot pots, **49**–50
foam pads, 56, 58
food. See also cook fires, about; cook fires, types of; cooking; cooking, and fires; cooking equipment; cookstoves, two-burner; eating; recipes
  for backpacking, 127, 129
  beverage ideas and tips, 154
  breakfast ideas and tips, 154
  containers for, 106
  dessert ideas and tips, 155
  developing a food plan, 88–89
  foraging for, 115
  lunch and dinner ideas and tips, 154–55, 159
  preparation and storage checklist, 143–44
  safety precautions, 160
  snack ideas and tips, 155
footwear, 65, 66–**67**, 112
Friday pack-and-go planner, 88–89
fuzz sticks, **37**, 38

**G**
gear, maintaining. See maintaining gear
gear, sources for, 145–47
gloves, 66
government lands information, addresses for, 151